POLITICAL ANTHROPOLOGY

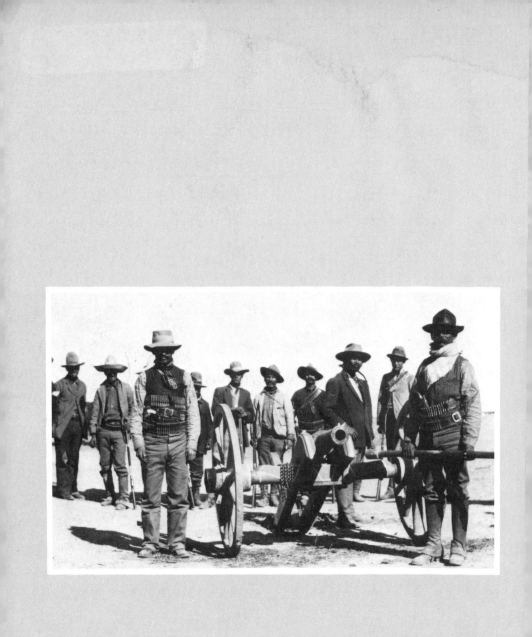

Political Anthropology

AN INTRODUCTION

Ted C. Lewellen

BERGIN & GARVEY
New York • Westport, Connecticut • London

Library of Congress Cataloging-in-Publication Data

Lewellen, Ted C., 1940-
    Political anthropology.

    Bibliography: p.
    Includes index.
    1. Political anthropology.   I. Title.
GN492.L48   1983   306'.2   82-22778
ISBN 0-89789-029-9 (pbk.)
ISBN 0-89789-028-0 (cl.)

Library of Congress Catalog Card Number: 82-22778
ISBN: 0-89789-028-0
ISBN: 0-89789-029-9 (pbk.)

First published in 1983

Bergin & Garvey, One Madison Avenue, New York, NY 10010
An imprint of Greenwood Publishing Group, Inc.

Printed in the United States of America

The paper used in this book complies with the
Permanent Paper Standard issued by the National
Information Standards Organization (Z39.48-1984).

10 9 8 7 6 5

Contents

Foreword

In this succinct and lucid account of the sporadic growth of political anthropology over the past four decades Ted Lewellen traces the development of its theoretical structure and the personal contributions of its main formulators. He makes available to the wider public of educated readers the issues, problems, perplexities, and achievements of political anthropologists as they have striven to make sense of the multitudinous ways in which societies on varying levels of scale and complexity handle order and dispute, both internal and external. He assesses the strength and probes the weaknesses of successive anthropological approaches to the study of political structures and processes, viewed both cross-culturally and in terms of intensive case studies. The result is a commendable guide to the varied sources of this increasingly important subdiscipline, a guide which, as far as I know, is unique of its kind; his criticisms are sharp, his style is genial, and his judgments just. As a student of the first generation of British political anthropologists of the structural-functionalist school, and a teacher of the medial generation of American political anthropologists, I can vouch for the accuracy and balance of Professor Lewellen's conclusions, and applaud the penetration of his criticisms, even when they are directed at positions promoted by those of my own theoretical persuasion.

Professor Lewellen states candidly that he has not written a textbook. Indeed, most textbooks are bulkier and overcharged with disparate materials, mainly descriptive. But this concise book is theoretically fine-honed and minutely integrated. It seems to be the introduction to political anthropology that we have all been waiting for, the prism which accurately segregates the significant constituents. Not only students, but also seasoned scholars will find worth in it. It is at once a summation and a new start.

VICTOR TURNER
Department of Anthropology
University of Virginia

Introduction

In a 1959 review article, political scientist David Easton charged that political anthropology did not really exist because the practitioners of this nondiscipline had utterly failed to mark off the political system from other subsystems of society. The judgment was then generally accepted with the humble mortification proper to a young science being criticized by one much older and wiser. It was not until almost ten years later that anthropologists had gained sufficient confidence to protest that Easton had completely misunderstood the nature of political anthropology and had construed its greatest virtue into a vice (Bailey 1968; A.P. Cohen 1969; Southall 1974). In the societies in which anthropologists have traditionally worked, politics *cannot* be analytically isolated from kinship, religion, age-grade associations, secret societies, and so forth, because these are precisely the institutions through which power and authority are manifested; in many societies "government" simply does not exist. This recognition, and the specification of the manner in which the idiom of politics is expressed through the medium of apparently nonpolitical institutions, may be the primary contributions of anthropology to the study of comparative politics. Recently, political anthropologists have carried this idea into the sacred domain of the political scientist by demonstrating that informal organizations and relationships may be more important than formal institutions even in such modern governments as those of the United States and Israel.

Nevertheless, Ronald Cohen, one of the most prolific researchers in the field, can still agree with Easton to the extent that "there are, as yet, no well-established conventions as to what [political anthropology] includes or excludes or what should be the basic methodological attack on the subject" (R. Cohen 1970: 484). This, unfortunately, remains as true today as it was ten years ago. In 1980, when I contracted to write the chapter on "Political Anthropology" for the *Handbook of Political Behavior* (Lewellen 1981), I set out, as I would for any such project, to search out a few overviews which could be compared and used as a guide to professional thinking on what constitutes the scope and subject matter of the discipline. This seemed a simple and obvious task: after all, there were three books actually titled *Political Anthropology* (Balandier 1970; Seaton & Claessen 1979; Swartz, Turner & Tuden 1966), entries on the subject in the *Annual Review of Anthropology* (Easton 1959; Vincent 1978; Winkler 1970) and the *Encyclopedia of the Social Sciences*, and chapters in every introductory anthropology textbook. However, what should have been a routine matter turned out to be an impossible one.

Despite the fact that political anthropology was already a thoroughly established subdiscipline of cultural anthropology—recognized within the field for almost four decades and taught at either the undergraduate or graduate level in many, if not most, colleges with anthropology departments—no real overview existed, anywhere.

To be sure, there were a number of quite good summary articles, but they were relatively narrow in scope, usually concentrating on one or another aspect of modern "process theory." Cultural anthropology textbooks, on the other hand, tended to focus, often exclusively, on the classification of preindustrial political systems, although most anthropologists abandoned that sort of thing long ago. The evolution of political systems, certainly a central concern, was too often relegated to the archeologists and sometimes seemed to be developing as a separate subdiscipline in itself. One got the impression that political anthropology was either extremely parochial in its interests or so vast and diffuse that it could not be delimited in a single overview.

Indeed, one problem with a book such as this is that it might give the reader the impression that the field is more coherent than is actually the case. Though a handful of researchers—notably Ronald Cohen, Abner Cohen, Elman Service, Georges Balandier, and F.G. Bailey—are self-consciously "political anthropologists," most articles in the field are by cultural anthropologists writing *about* politics. The result is that political anthropology exists largely through a potpourri of studies that can be classified within a few broad themes only with some effort and not a little artifice.

This said, a number of major thrusts of political anthropology can be legitimately delineated. First is the *classification of political systems.* Much of the early enthusiasm for creating ever more refined taxonomies has passed, but this continues to be an area of ongoing controversy. Secondly, the *evolution* of political systems is a continuing fascination in the United States, though British and French anthropologists often like to pretend that evolutionary theory died with Lewis Henry Morgan. Third is the study of the *structure and functions* of political systems in preindustrial societies. This point of view was vehemently repudiated on both sides of the Atlantic because of its static and ideal nature, but after the initial burst of revolutionary rhetoric there emerged a general recognition that even the most dynamic of political processes may take place within relatively stable structural boundaries. In any case, political anthropology had its beginnings in this paradigm, and many of its enduring works are structural-functionalist. Fourth, for the last two decades the theoretical focus has been on the *processes* of politics in preindustrial or developing societies. Perhaps the most assertive trend today is *action,* an outgrowth of the process approach with an emphasis not on changing institutions but on the manipulative strategies of individuals. Finally, there is a wide and growing literature on the *modernization* of formerly tribal societies and on modern political institutions in industrial states.

Beyond these minimal "themes," political anthropology shares a set of common values and assumptions that seem rooted in the nature of anthropology itself.

The Anthropological Perspective

In their introduction to *African Political Systems* (1940), generally considered the foundation work in political anthropology, Meyer Fortes and E.E. Evans-Pritchard stated flatly, "We have not found that the theories of political philosophers have helped us to understand the societies we have studied and we consider them of little scientific value. . ." (p. i). This sentiment might well have been the slogan of political anthropology in its developmental period. Until the mid-1960s, the theoretical framework of political anthropology, its methodology, its vocabulary, and its focus of interest owed little to political science, political sociology, or political psychology. In articles written before 1960, one might encounter an occasional reference to Hegel, Marx, Simmel, Parsons, or Easton, but by and large anthropologists remained blissfully untrained in political science, and their point of view was resolutely anthropological. This has changed as anthropologists turn increasingly to the study of modern nation-states and begin to assimilate systems theory and decision-models brought in from other disciplines. In many ways, however, political anthropology continues to be as much "anthropology" as "political."

Above all, anthropology is based on field experience. Individual researchers working in intense interaction with natives in their day-to-day setting seek to find—in the words of Ralph Nicholas—"order in the chaos of many people doing many things with many meanings" (Nicholas 1966:49). This disarmingly simple goal turns out to be tremendously complex. The closer one is to real people in natural settings, the harder it is to make generalizations about their behavior. This has led to a form of argument called "Bongo-Bongoism": no matter what generalization is made, someone will always be able to protest, "Ah, but in the Bongo Bongo tribe they do it differently." It is probably safe to say that there is always a Bongo Bongo tribe threatening at the periphery of every theorist's consciousness.

The result is that anthropology is decidedly *inductive* and *comparative*. Ideally, general theory should evolve from field data and should be so stated that it can be cross-culturally compared and analyzed. The founders of political anthropology quickly perceived that concepts derived from studies of the United States or Western Europe had little application to hunting-gathering bands or horticultural tribes.

Most American introductory textbooks in anthropology suggest the concept of "culture" as basic to the anthropological study of living social systems, but this is somewhat ethnocentric. Neither the British nor the French are particularly concerned with this rather ambiguous concept, and many American materialist and ecology-oriented theorists ignore it completely. Perhaps more useful is the concept of *adaptation*. Explicit or implicit in almost all anthropological writing is the idea that the people in question are making *rational adaptive responses* to their surroundings. This is not to say that the best adaptation is always made, or that certain institutions cannot be maladaptive (if the whole society were maladaptive, it would not survive), but social systems are never arbitrary.

Another important concept, deriving from early studies of "primitive" peoples who had little specialization of labor or of institutions, is that societies are comprised of interwoven networks of relations, so that a change in one element will affect the others. While this is no longer interpreted as rigidly as it once was—the relative autonomy of some subgroups is well documented—the idea of society as an integrated *system* remains fundamental to the anthropological perspective. Because the experimental sciences have been using two-part causal models for so long, one sometimes gets the impression that the concept of "system" is a recent discovery. Yet since the mid-nineteenth century, anthropologists have consistently and unselfconsciously studied societies as systems. It is true that the cross-cultural testing of hypotheses requires isolating discrete units from their cultural context, but in its statistical form this is a fairly late development, and it is generally used in a systemic framework. All the major paradigms in anthropology—evolutionary theory, the various functionalisms, French Structuralism, process theory, decision-theory, etc.—are basically "systems theories."

Finally, the theme of *evolution*, while periodically banished from social anthropology with great fanfare, remains an implicit assumption underlying even the most synchronic of paradigms. The reason is that anthropology deals with societies representing a wide spectrum in technological and social development, and it is virtually impossible to view these except along some scale of cultural complexity.

Induction, cross-cultural comparison, adaptation, system, and *evolution* are not really defining qualities of anthropology so much as various aspects of the anthropological way of looking at the world. While these provide a unified point of view, it is one that is at the same time replete with contradictions. Anthropologists seek no less than an understanding of the nature of humankind, yet they are suspicious of any generalization at all. They idealize a holistic view; yet, by the very complexity of the systems they confront, they are forced to isolate small subsystems. They demand precise classification, yet may argue that any typology at all distorts more than it clarifies. In sum, anthropologists are torn between diametrically opposed demands: to be true to the intense particularity of their field experience, and to give meaning to that experience by generalizing it to the world at large. This antithesis is a theme that runs through all of political anthropology.

   This book is written for anyone seeking a relatively painless overview of one of anthropology's most fascinating areas of specialization. I emphasize "painless" because this book is not a scholarly monograph nor a "state of the art" summary nor, heaven forbid, a "survey of the literature." Rather, I have tried to write the type of introduction to the subject that I would have welcomed as a student in a class on political anthropology—a book that provides the background necessary to understand the more focused ethnographic and theoretical accounts, as a stage setting might provide the context and meaning for a play's action. While the book may be read easily by undergraduates, professionals (including those outside the field of anthropology) should not be frightened off; I am offering here other people's research, and while the mode of presentation may be simplified, many of the ideas are both complex and insightful. If this book does no more than convey enough of the excitement of this frontier discipline to direct readers to the "real thing," I will be satisfied.

   The University of Richmond provided two faculty grants that made the research and writing of this book possible. Sam Long, editor of the multivolume *Handbook of Political Behavior,* recruited me into the project and overcame my original qualms. Plenum Press, publishers of the *Handbook,* were kind enough to give me permission to use about half of my original article (published in vol. 3) in this book. All deserve my sincerest thanks.

CHAPTER *1*

The Development of Political Anthropology

Though political anthropology as a specialization within social anthropology did not appear until as late as 1940, and did not really "kick in" until after World War II, this is also true for most anthropological subject specializations. From its beginnings as a scientific discipline in the latter half of the nineteenth century to the middle of the twentieth, anthropology was relatively unified. The early evolutionists admitted no boundaries to their comparative method and blithely roamed through the world and through the farther reaches of history examining any subject that met their eye. Franz Boas, the "Father of American Anthropology," was equally ready to analyze Eskimo art, Kwakiutl economics, or immigrant craniums. What lines were drawn were theoretical: one was an evolutionist, a historical particularist, a structural-functionalist, and so forth, but there was little sense that one might be a political anthropologist, an ethnolinguist, or an ecological anthropologist. The ideal of a holistic anthropology only began to break down through the forties as increasing data and increasing numbers of professional anthropologists forced specialization. The development of political anthropology was part of this general process, which continues today, with ever smaller subspecialties

1

being delineated. Yet the comparative study of politics in "primitive" societies dates to the very beginnings of anthropology.

The Nineteenth Century Evolutionists

Darwin's influence dominated the development of cultural anthropology in the second half of the nineteenth century just as it dominated biology. Much of the evolutionary theory emerging from this period was as primitive as the societies it sought to make sense of: evolutionary schemas were rigid and simplistic; there were endless arguments over whether the earliest societies were matriarchal or patriarchal; ethnocentrism ran rampant as Christianity and the Aryan "race" were seen as the ultimate developments of human progress; customs were torn out of their cultural context and compared indiscriminately by "armchair anthropologists" who had never seen the "savages" that were their subjects. Yet it is easy to forget how perceptive many of these studies were. Whatever their faults, the evolutionists laid the foundation for modern scientific anthropology (see Fig. 1).

Prior to this period, the tradition which reached back to Plato and ran through Aristotle, Hobbes, Rousseau, and most philosophers of politics until (but not including) Marx was that government and politics were products of civilization, and lower stages were characterized by anarchy. One of the earliest to challenge this view with hard evidence was Sir Henry Maine, who, in *Ancient Law* (1861), postulated that primitive society was organized along the lines of kinship, was patriarchal, and was ordered by sacred proscriptions. Evolution was in the direction of secularization and organization based not on kinship but on territory—"local contiguity"—which formed the basis for political action.

Maine's important insight that kinship could be a primary sociopolitical structure was developed by Louis Henry Morgan in *Ancient Society* (1877). Morgan had studied the Iroquois Indians of New York state first hand and had been fascinated by their kinship terminology, which was very different from that used in Western European countries but similar to that employed in other parts of the world. His description and categorization of kinship systems was itself a lasting contribution, but before these could gain recognition they had to be couched in the type of theoretical framework popular at the time. Morgan developed an evolutionary sequence based on mode of subsistence, the stages of which he termed "savagery," "barbarism," and "civilization." These grossly connotative terms actually translate rather well into their modern equivalents, societies based on hunting/gathering, horticulture, and developed agricul-

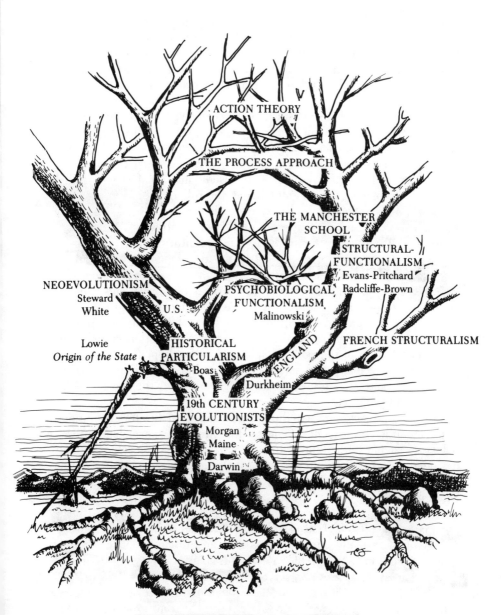

Fig. 1   Political Anthropology Family Tree

ture. Morgan, like others of his time, began with the "postulate of the psychic unity of mankind"—the belief that there was a common origin and parallel development all over the world—though he was unable to follow the idea to its inherently antiracist conclusions and assumed that the Aryans were naturally "in the central stream of human progress" (Morgan 1877:533).

With his considerable sophistication in the analysis of kinship, Morgan was able to elaborate Maine's inchoate ideas. Social organization began with the "promiscuous horde" which developed into kin-based units, organized along sexual lines—namely, intermarrying sets of male siblings and female siblings (this was an early insight into what is now called "cross-cousin marriage"). In emphasizing the role of exogamy (marriage outside the social group) he touched on the conception of intergroup bonds formed through marriage that would become the "alliance theory" of French structuralists three-quarters of a century later. Progressive restriction of marriage partners led to the development of gens (i.e., clans) which joined to create increasingly larger units up to a confederacy of tribes. Sociopolitical structure at this level is egalitarian and is based on sets of interpersonal relations. (With the exception of the "promiscuous horde," this is not a bad description of the Iroquois confederacy, though there is little reason to generalize to a universal evolutionary process). The specialization of the political sphere does not appear until the full domestication of plants and animals creates sufficient surplus to lead to urbanization and private property. True government, then, is based on territory and property.

Morgan is subject to most of the criticisms directed by later generations at the evolutionists (except, of course, that he was no "armchair anthropologist," having studied the Iroquois first hand). Yet much of his thinking has been absorbed into modern anthropology. This is especially true in relation to politics. Though anthropologists no longer distinguish kin-based from territory-based groups (all people recognize territorial boundaries), Morgan's emphasis on kinship as a primary medium of political articulation at the subsistence levels of hunting/gathering and horticulture was justified. Equally important was Morgan's discovery of the "gens" as a corporate lineage in which decision-making was confined within a group tracing common ancestry through either the male or the female line. Another lasting insight was his recognition of the egalitarianism of primitive society and the lack of a concept of private property. These latter ideas contributed to Morgan's most effective influence: they formed the basis for Frederick Engels's *The Origin of the Family, Private Property and the State* (1891/1972), the Marxian view of the evolution of capitalism.

The Reaction

Early twentieth-century anthropology was characterized by two fundamental changes: the rejection of evolutionary theory and methodology,
and a widening hiatus between the anthropologies of the United States
and of England and France. In the latter countries, the immediate repudiation of evolutionism was relatively mild, but there was a significant
shift in new directions. This shift was based on the work of Emile Durkheim—in France leading to an increasingly cognitive structuralism that
would culminate with the works of Claude Lévi-Strauss, in England leading to an emphasis on "social facts" (and a corresponding disregard for
the psychological aspect of culture) and a theoretical point of view dominated by the ideas of "function" and "structure." Durkheim had little
influence on U.S. "cultural anthropology," where Franz Boas's "historical
particularism" dominated. Boas was absolute, and often vehement, in his
repudiation of the comparative method and of the vast generalizations
that had emerged from it. He emphasized minute descriptive studies of
particular cultures. Theory did not disappear altogether, but such orientations as "diffusionism" took on a very particularistic turn, with field
anthropologists spending years collecting the most miniscule facts of daily
life and charting them on enormous trait lists (one suspects this type of
inquiry declined through sheer boredom). Though English anthropologists were turning increasingly to the study of kinship, not much was
accomplished in terms of the political dimension, aside from an occasional
reference to Durkheim's "mechanical" and "organic" solidarity. In the
United States there was little in the way of theory that would separate
out the political for analysis.

A major exception was Robert Lowie's *The Origin of the State* (1927).
In order to find a framework to deal with the political, Lowie reached
back to outmoded evolutionary theory. Fittingly enough, he started by
rejecting the unilineal evolution of his predecessors; there was no evidence that all societies pass through similar stages of development.
Maine's and Morgan's contention that primitive political order was maintained solely through personal relations was also rejected. Rather, the
territorial bond, which Morgan saw as a characteristic of civilization, was
universal, and thus formed a bridge between primitive political organization and the state. In an earlier book, *Primitive Society* (1920), Lowie
had recognized the political importance of associations in uniting otherwise disparate groups and he saw these as forming the basis of the state
because they weakened the blood ties of kin groups. Now he modified
this view, showing how associations can also be as "separatistic" as kin
relations. Thus associations, which are of their nature neither centralizing

nor disruptive, require a supra-ordinate authority in order to achieve higher level integration.

Georges Balandier's (1970) recent contention that specific, explicit political anthropology developed during the twenties is true only to a point. Here we find certain lasting ideas: that all societies recognize territory, that increases in population and in conflict lead to states, that class stratification is a key element in movement up the evolutionary ladder toward the state, and that the central element of the state is a monopoly of coercive power. Though these concepts were not developed in a systematic causal model, Lowie clarified a number of issues, asked a number of crucial questions, and presented anthropology with a fascinating challenge.

Unfortunately, the challenge was not taken up. The evolutionary phrasing of Lowie's book, despite his denials of unilineal development, must have seemed sadly anachronistic to his peers who had thought themselves done with this evolutionary nonsense once and for all. The beginning of political anthropology was also its end—until 1940.

The British Functionalists

In England during the thirties two brands of functionalism vied for dominance—one, the "psychobiological functionalism" of Bronislaw Malinowski, the other the "structural-functionalism" of A. R. Radcliffe-Brown. Malinowski, often considered the founder of modern fieldwork techniques for his extensive research in the Trobriand Islands, sought to interpret cultural institutions as derived from certain psychological and biological needs. Though he contributed little to political anthropology per se, his studies of law, economics and religion—as observed in ongoing, rather than historical, society—cleared the way for the type of specialization that would later become commonplace. Malinowski's "participant observation" method became the model for an entire generation of British fieldworkers whose intense analyses of African societies would establish political anthropology as a legitimate subdiscipline. However, it was Radcliffe Brown's "structural" brand of functionalism which would ultimately come to predominate in England, where academic chairmanships at Oxford, London, or Manchester were close to the equivalent of theoretical fiefdoms. For Radcliffe-Brown, a society was an equilibrium system in which each part functioned to the maintenance of the whole (the obvious organic analogy was not avoided). Thus there was a sense that societies were to be described from high above, to be mapped to show how their various elements intermeshed. As we shall see, this approach is more atemporal than static—that is, it does not really postulate an unchanging society or a society without conflict, but rather its focus is on those norms, values, and ideal structures that form the framework within which activity takes place.

Feeding this theoretical orientation, and feeding upon it, was the concentration of British research in colonial Africa. Much of the purpose of such research was to instruct colonial authorities on the social systems under their control, and this affected both the emphasis and the image of social anthropology. On the one hand, there was little recognition that the societies anthropologists were studying were severely changed by colonialism, and by the *Pax* Britannica imposed by English guns. Also, there was a tendency to study chiefdom and state systems, some of which, like the Zulu, had been integrated partially as a reaction to the British threat.

These two trends, structural-functionalism and the African experience, came together in 1940 in a work which, at a single blow, established modern political anthropology: *African Political Systems*, edited by Meyer Fortes and E.E. Evans-Pritchard. In their introduction, the editors distinguish two types of African political system: those with centralized authority and judicial institutions (primitive states), and those without such authority and institutions (stateless societies). A major difference between these types is the role of kinship. Integration and decision-making in stateless societies is, at the lowest level, based on bilateral family/band groups and, on a higher level, on corporate unilineal descent groups. State societies are those in which an administrative organization overrides or unites such groups as the permanent basis of political structure. This typology was later criticized as much too simplistic, but the detailed descriptions of how lineages functioned politically in several specific societies were lasting contributions. Social equilibrium was assumed, so that the major problem was to show how the various conflict and interest groups maintained a balance of forces that resulted in a stable, ongoing social structure. The integrating power of religion and symbol were also noted, especially the role of ritual in confirming and consolidating group values.

African Political Systems' introduction and eight ethnographic articles established the problems, the theoretical foundation, the methodology, and the controversy for more than a decade of research into the politics of preindustrial societies. The original typology was increasingly refined. For example, A.L. Southall in *Alur Society* (1953) challenged the assumption that segmentary systems—those in which authority was dispersed among a number of groups—were always uncentralized; he provided an example of a society in which segmentary lineage organization existed side-by-side with a centralized state. Others questioned segmentation as a factor for typing at all, since even centralized governments are segmented. Nor could lineages be the basis for all stateless societies, since age grades, secret associations, and ritual groups could cross-cut lineage divisions for purposes of political action. Jumping off from Fortes and Evans-Pritchard's bare suggestion of types (the two editors did not seem to think their typology universal, or even very important), classifications were increasingly refined until political taxonomy became virtually an autonomous field of research. The static structural-functionalist paradigm maintained itself through a number of studies as the old guard—Evans-Pritchard, Raymond Firth, Daryll Forde, and Meyer Fortes—held, contemporaneously or successively, the princely academic chairs of British anthropology. This is not to say that the situation itself was static; there was constant ferment, as Malinowskian or Radcliffe-Brownian emphases alternated, and as conflict and change increasingly imposed themselves with the rapid demise of African colonialism.

The Transition

By the mid-fifties, after a decade of gradual chipping away, the edifice of structural-functionalism was showing cracks in its very foundation. There was little sense yet of a complete repudiation of this paradigm, but there was a quite self-conscious sense that fundamental modifications were being made.

A major contribution in this direction was Edmund Leach's *Political Systems of Highland Burma* (1954), which signalled the shift to a more process-oriented, more dynamic form of analysis. In the Kachin Hills area of Burma, Leach found not one but three different types of political system: a virtually anarchic system of the *gumlao* Kachin, an unstable and intermediate *gumsa* system, and a small-scale centralized Shan state. The Kachin and Shan were more or less distinct communities, which in turn were made up of many linguistic, cultural, and political subgroups, all somehow forming an interrelated whole. The system could not be supposed to be in equilibrium; indeed, *gumsa* and *gumlao* seemed to change into one another. In order to make sense out of all this, Leach felt it necessary to "force these facts within the constraining mold of an *as if* system of ideas, composed of concepts which are treated *as if* they are part of an equilibrium system" (Leach 1954:ix). This was no more than the people themselves did, for they also had an ideal cognitive pattern for their society, expressed in ritual and symbolism. In reality, however, the people were hardly constrained to follow their own, and certainly not the anthropologist's, *as if* conception of their behavior. These ideas are similar to the mentalistic structuralism of Claude Lévi-Strauss (whom Leach would later help introduce into English-language anthropology), and there are suggestions of the "cognitive mapping" later to become central to American psychological anthropology. The immediate importance for the study of politics, however, was in the clear differentiation of abstract political structure from the on-the-ground political reality. Almost as crucial, Leach finally got political anthropology out of Africa and broke it free from the relatively cohesive, single-language societies to which it had been confined.

Meanwhile, Max Gluckman was also breaking new ground. In his chapter on the Zulu in *African Political Systems*, in *Custom and Conflict in Africa* (1956), and in *Order and Rebellion in Tribal Africa* (1960), Gluckman developed the theme that equilibrium is neither static nor stable, but grows out of an ongoing dialectical process in which conflicts within one set of relations are absorbed and integrated within another set of relations: cross-cutting loyalties tend to unite the wider society in settling a feud between local groups; witchcraft accusations displace hostilities within a group in a way that does not threaten the system; *apartheid* in South Africa, while radically dividing White from Black, ultimately unites both groups within themselves. The Roman maxim "divide and conquer" is cleverly restated as "divide and cohere." Politically, this is especially evident in African rituals of rebellion in which, periodically, the king must dress as a pauper or act the clown, is symbolically killed, or is subjected to open hatred and obscenities from his people. For Gluckman, such rituals are not merely catharsis; they are the symbolic reassertion of the priority of the system over the individual, of kingship over any particular king.

At this stage, both Leach and Gluckman are transitional figures, still rooted in the structural-functionalism of the 1930s and 1940s, developing ever more clever arguments in defense of equilibrium theory; yet at the same time they are taking a giant step toward a new paradigm. Gluckman, as founder and chairman of the anthropology department at Manchester University, was to see his ideas extensively elaborated by his students, known collectively as the "Manchester School," a phrase that came to represent a new orientation to society based not on structure and function but on process and conflict.

The Neo-Evolutionists

Without a doubt, England dominated political anthropology during its first two decades. Meanwhile, in the United States, an incipient and quite different political anthropology was fermenting. Evolutionism, long banned by Boasian edict from the proper study of mankind, began a slow and not entirely respectable resurgence through the writings of Leslie White and Julian Steward. White (1943, 1959) developed a complex sequence leading through agricultural intensification to private ownership, specialization, class stratification, political centralization, and so forth. Much of this was elucidated at such a high level of generality that it left White open to the charge of merely resuscitating nineteenth-century unilineal theory, and Steward's (1965) use of the term "multilinear" evolution for his own theory only served to validate an unnecessary dichotomy. Actually, no serious evolutionist has ever held a truly unilineal theory (Harris 1968:171–173). But the situation was not clarified until the unilineal-multilineal dichotomy was replaced with the complementary concepts of "general" evolution and "specific" evolution, the higher level referring to evolutionary processes such as increased specialization or intensification of production, the lower to the historic sequence of forms (Sahlins & Service 1960). This clarified, evolutionary anthropology was free to move, unfettered by a heavy load of semantic, rather than substantive, difficulties.

Thus, in contrast to their English colleagues, American political anthropologists *started* with the idea of change—on a panoramic scale—in a context that was fundamentally ecological and materialist. White measures evolution in terms of energy efficiency and sees technology as prime mover. Steward's "cultural ecology" focused on the "cultural core" — mainly, the subsistence and economic arrangements which largely determine social structure and ideology. The differences between British and American anthropology were vast, but can be overemphasized. For example, one of the earliest American political ethnographies, E. Adamson Hoebel's 1940 study of the Comanche Indians, was neither evolutionary nor materialist. Throughout the 1940s and 1950s, and into the 1960s, there was a strong current of structural-functionalism in the United States. But that which was *particularly* American was vastly different from that which was *particularly* British, to the extent that there was often little communication between the two.

Political evolution quickly became almost synonymous with political classification. The two major evolutionary works of the period, Elman Service's *Primitive Social Organization* (1962) and Morton Fried's *The Evolution of Political Society* (1967), were more taxonomic and descriptive than causal; the emphasis was on the characteristics of different levels of sociocultural integration, rather than on the factors that caused evolution from one level to another. Causal theories were hardly lacking, but these derived from archeology rather than cultural anthropology. Many notable archeologists devoted their careers to the processes involved in the evolution of state societies. These two trends, the archeological and the cultural, which originally ran parallel, came together in Service's *Origins of the State and Civilization* (1975). Political evolution remains an ongoing field of study, but it can no longer claim to be the major focus of American political anthropology—process and decision-making orientations have crossed the Atlantic from England.

Process and Decision-Making

Max Gluckman had tentatively experimented with the analysis of "situations" involving individuals, in contrast to the usual ethnographic focus on group norms and social structures. Elaborating on this experiment, Victor Turner, in *Schism and Continuity in an African Society* (1957), followed a single individual through a series of "social dramas" in which personal and community manipulations of norms and values were laid bare. To Gluckman and Leach's emphasis on process and conflict was added a new element—individual decision making observed in crisis situations.

The belated discovery that the world is in motion stimulated an enthusiastic disavowal of structural-functionalism, almost equal to that which had temporarily obliterated evolutionism at the turn of the century. "Structure" and "function" became unfashionable terms, to be replaced by "process," "conflict," "faction," "struggle," "manipulative strategy," and the like. As Janet Bujra succinctly expressed it:

> For the early functionalist, the assumption was that social unity was the normal state of affairs, whereas conflict was a problematic situation which could not easily be incorporated into their theoretical framework. More recent studies of political behavior, however, seem to indicate that it is conflict which is the norm, and it is the existence of social unity which is more difficult to explain [Bujra 1973:43].

That conflict and accord, unity and disunity, might be two sides of the same coin, as Gluckman emphasized, was temporarily forgotten.

The change from structural theory to process theory had its objective correlate in the dissolution of the false stability imposed by colonialism in Africa. With the rise of post-colonial nation states, and the incorporation of tribal societies within larger political organizations, new problems presented themselves. No longer could "primitive" politics be treated as though it existed in a closed system; the wider socio-political "field" replaced the more restricted concept of political "system." On the other hand, the intensive study of particular situations gave rise to the more restricted concept of political "arena," wherein individuals and political teams vie for power and leadership.

Though many of these ideas come together in such works as Balandier's *Political Anthropology* (1970) and Swartz, Turner and Tuden's Introduction to their edited volume of the same title (1966), it would be a mistake to consider the process approach as a coherent theory. Many ethnographies that emphasize process continue to focus on the level of norms and institutions. The individual-focused, decision-making approach—often referred to as "action theory"—is a somewhat separate subdivision of the less cohesive process orientation.

Process theory has opened the way for a cross-Atlantic dialogue that was muted, at best, during the heyday of structural-functionalism. Such American leaders of political anthropology as Marc Swartz and Ronald Cohen have shown only passing interest in evolution or evolutionary typology, but have joined the British in what now constitutes a truly international trend, one that is proving itself useful not only for the analysis of the politics of tribal groups but also for that of modern industrial states.

SUGGESTED READINGS

Harris, Marvin
The Rise of Anthropological Theory (New York: Thomas Crowell, 1968)
Harris's relentlessly materialistic orientation can be infuriating when applied to theories for which he has no sympathy. Nevertheless, this massive work is impressive in its scope and scholarship and entertaining even when one disagrees with the analysis. Though Harris does not deal separately with political anthropology, he provides the context within which political anthropology must be understood.

Kuper, Adam
Anthropologists and Anthropology: The British School 1922–1972 (New York: Pica Press, 1973)
Political anthropology had its origins in British structural-functionalism. I know of no book that presents a clearer overview of this school and its critics. Also, there are fascinating biographies and character portraits of such luminaries as E.E. Evans-Pritchard, E.R. Leach, and Max Gluckman.

Mair, Lucy
Primitive Government (Bloomington: Indiana University Press, 1962)
This book, which deals entirely with Africa, is one of the few works to attempt a general overview of politics in preindustrial societies from the point of view of British structuralism. However, the author's generalizatons sometimes get lost in the myriad examples, which follow one upon the other with confusing rapidity.

Traditional Eskimo society is made up of egalitarian bands that fluctuate in size according to the seasonal availability of food (Library of Congress).

CHAPTER 2

Types of Preindustrial Political Systems

No anthropologist lays himself more open to the threat of "Bongo-Bongoism" than he who dares to classify. (As you will recall, whatever generalization is made in the field of anthropology, some researcher will be able to protest, "Ah, but in the Bongo Bongo tribe they do it differently.") It is safe to say that when it comes to creating typologies of social systems, such aberrant tribes abound. One noted British anthropologist, Edmund Leach, once relegated virtually all attempts at anthropological classification to the lowly status of "butterfly collecting, on the grounds that the resulting typologies made no more sense than, say, grouping together all blue butterflies" (Leach 1961).

Though a few political anthropologists might unhesitatingly agree, classification has been a major focus of research ever since politics was separated out as a subsystem worthy of specific attention. The results of forty years of the increasing refinement of political types will completely satisfy no one, but this is as one might expect when something as fluid and unpredictable as society is confined within a set of neat pigeon holes. Yet, surprisingly, a general system of classification has been more or less agreed upon, as shown in Figure 2, and this system seems vindicated by quantitative cross-cultural testing. This synthetic classification shown in

15

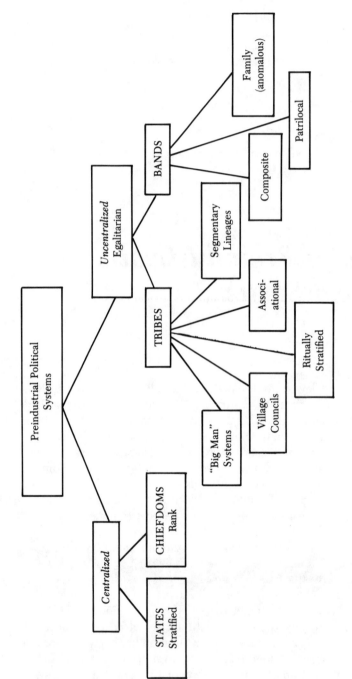

Fig. 2 *Preindustrial Political Systems*

SOURCES: Eisenstadt 1959; Fried 1967; Service 1971.

Figure 2 is based on means of political integration, access to leadership positions, and method of group decision making. Centralized systems seem relatively uniform by these criteria; but if other criteria are used, many subtypes are possible. A classification of "early" states based on degree of complexity appears as Table 3 (p. 60).

Such classification is possible because a society is no more just a collection of individual human beings than a house is just a conglomeration of lumber, bricks and nails. Two houses built of different materials but to the same floor plan will obviously be much more alike than two houses of the same materials but very different designs (say, a town house and a ranch house). Similarly, we would not expect to find the same architecture in the arctic and in the tropics, nor among the pastoral Nuer of Africa and the modern industrial Swedes. In short, a house is defined in terms of its organization, not its components, and that organization will be influenced by its physical environment and the level of technology of the people who designed it.

The analogy can be strained, but it helps to keep some such idea in mind when dealing with any type of anthropological classification. If we are to place the Bushmen of the Kalahari Desert of Africa in the same political category ("bands") as the nineteenth-century Shoshone Indians of Utah, it must be on the assumption that a hunting-gathering adaptation to an arid environment gives rise to particular social characteristics, such as egalitarian groups with no formal leadership and a system of economic exchange based on sharing. The relationships are causal, to be sure, but it is more difficult than one might think to determine exactly how one element of a system "causes" another. Does the arid environment, and thus the relative scarcity of food and water, cause low population densities and consequently a flexible small-group type of social organization? Perhaps. But we usually think of a cause as being active, whereas the "environment" just sort of sits there. Besides, the relationship between society and environment is one of constant feedback; people not only adapt to their surroundings but also change their physical and social worlds to meet their own needs. In other words, when classifying social systems it is often more productive to think in terms of structural relationships, in the sense that one element logically implies another. A useful typology, then, would be one that delineates *systems*, that is, units in which the parts are so structurally interrelated that from the specification of one element we can predict other elements.

However, it cannot be too strongly emphasized that interrelations of social traits (e.g., chiefdoms and unilineal kinship) represent only statistical probabilities. To return to our house analogy, we might find that "ranch" houses can be legitimately classed together, but we would also expect an enormous range of variation of particulars within the general style. In contrast to strictly materialist theories of culture, environment and technology do not seem so much to *determine* social structure and ideology as to *limit* the range of possibilities.

Table 1 suggests some of the social and economic characteristics we might reasonably associate with each major political type. Any such chart must be approached with caution. First, no society should be expected to match all the characteristics of its type, any more than we would expect to discover some perfectly average American who is five-foot-ten, weighs 175, is Protestant, earns $13,275 per year, and has 1.44 children. Second, what this chart really shows is "cultural complexity," and therefore one should not assume that political type is the primary determinant because the major headings are "band," "tribe," "chiefdom," and "state"; if this book were about kinship instead of politics, the headings might just as well be "bilateral," "patrilineal," "matrilineal," etc. Third, it must be kept in mind that certain characteristics are better predictors than others. Oddly enough, subsistence level is a very *poor* predictor of social organization. Statistically, the strongest predictor of political type, kinship, religion, and the like is *population density* (which is not included on the chart, since increasing densities from band through state may be assumed). Fourth, a chart of this kind, by its very nature, implies that each of these types is quite distinct from the others, whereas in reality these types form points along a continuum. Fifth, it should neither be assumed that a higher level of cultural complexity leaves behind all the characteristics of lower levels (reciprocity, for example, is a significant means of exchange in all societies) nor that cultural complexity is simply additive (bilateral systems of kinship appear at both the simplest and most complex levels but are replaced by unilineal kinship at the intermediate levels). Finally, special mention must be made of the case of religion, where we find a strong relation between cultural complexity and religious organization, but little or no relation in regard to belief (which is why magic, animism, polytheism, monotheism, etc., are not mentioned on the chart). If these *caveats* are kept in mind, the chart provides a useful summary of the characteristics of preindustrial political systems.

Uncentralized Systems

Many of the groups studied by anthropologists possess little that could be called "government," at least not in the sense of a permanent political elite. In most of these traditional systems, power is fragmentary and temporary, dispersed among families, bands, lineages, and various associations. Wider political groups may be formed temporarily to counter some threat, such as warring neighbors, but these groups will break apart when the problem has been overcome. Thus these social systems can best be viewed not as permanent, centrally organized societies, but rather as fluid groups that, over short or long periods of time, sometimes seasonally and sometimes almost randomly, coalesce into larger "tribal" units then disintegrate into smaller units, which may themselves be divisible. While politics is constant in such societies as individuals seek support for leadership positions, as public decisions are made, and as territory is defended, it is not manifested in either a monopoly of coercive force or in any form of centralized economic system based on taxes or tribute. There may be great differences in individual status, but there is little in the way of class stratification, so these systems, while only egalitarian in any real sense at their lowest level—that of hunters-gatherers—do appear more "democratic" in decision making and access to leadership than more centralized groups.

Bands

A major conclusion deriving from a 1965 Conference on Band Organization was that the term "band," while still useful, was regularly applied to groups as diverse as those with an average size of 25, as well as those with 300 to 400 members, rendering the term virtually meaningless. It was also argued that the usual defining qualities of bands—seasonal scheduling, lack of centralized authority structures, and hunting-gathering economy—were not sufficiently restrictive to make these units automatically comparable (Damas 1968). However, in those few societies lacking agriculture, domesticated food animals, or dependable year-round fishing, there would seem to be only a limited number of cultural options available. Similarities in the social and political structures of such widely separated groups as the Canadian Eskimo and Australian Aborigines suggest that dependence on wild foods, the consequent nomadism, and seasonal redistributions of population fix the adaptive possibilities within relatively narrow limits. For this reason, the band was probably the normal mode of social organization in Paleolithic times.

Bands are typically small, with perhaps 25 to 150 individuals, grouped in nuclear families. While there is division of labor along age and sex lines, there is virtually no specialization of skills, with the result that the unity of the wider group is, in Emile Durkheim's term, "mechanical"— i.e., it is based on custom, tradition, and common values and symbols, rather than on an interdependence of specialized roles. A strict rule of

Table 1 Preindustrial Political Systems: An Evolutionary Typology

	Uncentralized		Centralized	
	Band	Tribe	Chiefdom	State
Type of Subsistence	Hunting-gathering; little or no domestication	Extensive agriculture (horticulture) and pastoralism	Extensive agriculture; intensive fishing	Intensive agriculture
Type of Leadership	Informal and situational leaders; may have a headman who acts as arbiter in group decision making	Charismatic headman with no "power" but some authority in group decision making	Charismatic chief with limited power based on bestowal of benefits on followers	Sovereign leader supported by an aristocratic bureaucracy
Type and Importance of Kinship	Bilateral kinship, with kin relations used differentially in changing size and composition of bands	Unilineal kinship (patrilineal or matrilineal) may form the basic structure of society	Unilineal, with some bilateral; descent groups are ranked in status	State demands supra-kinship loyalties; access to power is based on ranked kin groups, either unilineal or bilateral
Major Means of Social Integration	Marriage alliances unite larger groups; bands united by kinship and family; economic interdependence based on reciprocity	Pantribal sodalities based on kinship, voluntary associations and/or age-grades	Integration through loyalty to chief, ranked lineages, and voluntary associations	State loyalties supercede all lower-level loyalties; integration through commerce and specialization of function
Political Succession	May be hereditary headman, but actual leadership falls to those with special knowledge or abilities	No formal means of political succession	Chief's position not directly inherited, but chief must come from a high-ranking lineage	Direct hereditary succession of sovereign; increasing appointment of bureaucratic functionaries
Major Types of Economic Exchange	Reciprocity (sharing)	Reciprocity; trade may be more developed than in bands	Redistribution through chief; reciprocity at lower levels	Redistribution based on formal tribute and/or taxation; markets and trade

Social Stratification	Egalitarian	Egalitarian	Rank (individual and lineage)	Classes (minimally of rulers and ruled)
Ownership of Property	Little or no sense of personal ownership	Communal (lineage or clan) ownership of agricultural lands and cattle	Land communally owned by lineage, but strong sense of personal ownership of titles, names, privileges, ritual artifacts, etc.	Private and state ownership increases at the expense of communal ownership
Law and Legitimate Control of Force	No formal laws or punishments; right to use force is communal	No formal laws or punishments; right to use force belongs to lineage, clan, or association	May be informal laws and specified punishments for breaking taboos; chief has limited access to physical coercion	Formal laws and punishments; state holds all legitimate access to use of physical force
Religion	No religious priesthood or full-time specialists; shamanistic	Shamanistic; strong emphasis on initiation rites and other rites of passage that unite lineages	Inchoate formal priesthood; hierarchical, ancestor-based religion	Full-time priesthood provides sacral legitimization of state
Recent and Contemporary Examples	!Kung Bushmen (Africa) Pygmies (Africa) Eskimo (Canada, Alaska) Shoshone (U.S.)	Kpelle (W. Africa) Yanomamo (Venezuela) Nuer (Sudan) Cheyenne (U.S.)	Precolonial Hawaii Kwakiutl (Canada) Tikopia (Polynesia) Dagurs (Mongolia)	Ankole (Uganda) Jimma (Ethiopia) Kachari (India) Volta (Africa)
Historic and Prehistoric Examples	Virtually all paleolithic societies	Iroquois (U.S.), Oaxaca Valley (Mexico), 1500–1000 B.C.	Precolonial Ashanti, Benin, Dahomy (Africa) Scottish Highlanders	Precolonial Zulu (Africa) Aztec (Mexico) Inca (Peru) Sumeria (Iraq)

SOURCES: Abrahamson 1969; Carniero 1970; Eisenstadt 1959; Fried 1967; Levinson and Malone 1980; Lomax and Arensberg 1977; Service 1971.

band exogamy forces marriage alliances with other bands, and this wider group is typically united also by bilateral kinship (traced equally through both parents). Lineages, in the sense of corporate descent groups holding territorial rights, would not be sufficiently flexible for the constant fluctuations of hunting-gathering societies.

Morton Fried (1967) categorizes such groups as "egalitarian" in terms of economy, social organization, and political structure. Distribution of food and other needed goods is at the simplest level of sharing; bonds are established within the band and between bands on the basis of ongoing reciprocal relations. Political organization is also egalitarian to the extent that decision making is usually a group enterprise, and access to leadership positions is equally open to all males within a certain age range. Leadership, which is temporary, shifting according to the situation, is based on the personal attributes of the individual and lacks any coercive power. A headman or leader in a hunt cannot really tell anyone what to do, but must act as arbiter for the group, and perhaps as expert advisor in particular situations.

This least complex of political structures may be further subdivided into "patrilocal," "composite," and "anomalous" bands. The patrilocal type is based upon band exogamy and a marriage rule that the woman live with her husband's group. This type is so widespread that Elman Service regarded it as "almost an inevitable kind of organization" (Service 1962:97). Indeed, it has the advantage of band stability, since each group is constantly replenished over time by new members coming in from outside; but it also is capable of forming wide ranging alliances through marriage and possesses considerable flexibility. The composite band was viewed by Service as the result of the collapse of originally patrilocal structures that were rapidly depopulated from disease and war after having come in contact with civilization. It is a group which lacks either band exogamy or a marriage residence rule, and which is thus "more of an expedient agglomeration than a structured society." In the "anomalous" category are the Basin Shoshone and the Eskimo, both of which have social structures so fragmented that they have been characterized as typifying the "family level" of socio-cultural integration.

THE !KUNG BUSHMEN. The Nyae Nyae region of the Kalahari Desert in southwest Africa covers about 10,000 square miles, in which there are a number of small waterholes but no rivers or streams or other surface water except for some shallow ponds during a brief rainy season. Within this area, about 1,000 !Kung Bushmen (the "!" represents a "click" in their pronunciation) live in 36 or 37 bands. Though at the lowest level of technological development, relying on digging sticks and poison-tipped spears and carrying all of their meager possessions with them during their constant treks in search of food and water, they have adapted well to the extremely hostile environment. About 80 percent of the food is supplied by the women, who daily collect nuts, fruits, tubers, roots, and various other "field foods." The remainder of !Kung subsistence is supplied through hunting, which is exclusively a male occupation. Various species of large antelope provide most of the meat, though occasionally a buffalo or a giraffe may also be killed. About fifteen to eighteen such large animals are killed by a single band in a year, and the meat is shared by the entire group.

While there is no separate "political" sphere among the !Kung, a number of political problems must be dealt with, such as the defense of territories, the protection and allocation of water, and public goals in regard to band movements and collective hunts. Each band claims a territory that must have a permanent source of water at a reasonable distance from sufficient vegetable foods for day-to-day consumption. Within such a territory will be sporadic fertile areas, such as groves of mangetti nut trees, clumps of berries, and special places where tubers grow in particular abundance; these are considered "owned" by a band and are jealously guarded. Incursions into another band's territory occasionally occur, especially during hunting expeditions, in which case violence may be threatened; but true wars are unknown.

"Headmanship" is passed on from father to son. The existence of hereditary political positions defies our principle that nearly everyone in a band or egalitarian society has equal access to leadership. However, the headman's authority is largely limited to control of "field food" and water; he plans the utilization of these various resources and has charge of the group's movements from one area to another within the territory. Most of this is firmly established by custom, and important decisions will be arrived at by group consensus; so the headman position is to some extent symbolic. Visitors must ask his permission to partake of food or water within the band's territory, but custom dictates that all reasonable requests be granted. Headmanship brings responsibility without reward, and since it is also the !Kung ideal that no individual should stand above another, such positions are seldom actively sought.

The hereditary headman may or may not be the actual leader of the band. If he is too young or lacks leadership abilities, this role may fall to someone with more of the personal qualities of leadership, so that the "official" position becomes virtually nominal. Also, effective leadership shifts according to the situation: a person may be an exceptional hunt leader but have little authority over public decisions, such as when and where to move camp (Marshall 1967).

THE ESKIMO.   Despite the vast territory inhabited by the Eskimo (from Siberia to Greenland) they have been described as remarkably alike in their political and social organization. Environmental determinist arguments are especially tempting, for the Eskimo live in possibly the most hostile humanly-habitable regions on Earth. Their food resources—mainly fish, caribou, and seal (the Eskimo are the only existing hunting-gathering people who do not rely on vegetable foods)—are seasonal and widely scattered, which would logically lead to low population densities, nomadism, and extremely fluid social organization based on small subsistence units. This, in fact, is the way traditional Eskimo society has been depicted. The basic unit is the extended family, which can take advantage of bilateral kinship relations to join with other families in temporary bands or even villages as food supplies wax and wane during the year. A household might comprise a family of twelve, which subsists alone part of the year but joins groups of up to 270 at other times. Leadership outside the household is elementary; even villages sometimes lack a headman, and what minimal influence might be possessed by an individual will rest with the local shaman, whose authority is neither coercive nor uniting. Along the coast, the owner of a whaling boat has unrestricted authority over his crew during a voyage, and might, by the prestige of his wealth, maintain a loose chieftainship over a community; but even in this case group unity is maintained not by government but by conventionalized reciprocal obligations among kin. As with the !Kung, maintenance of order derives from the power of custom and public opinion (Weyer 1959).

While this textbook view of the Eskimo is probably reasonably accurate for a majority of groups, recent research reveals a much greater diversity of traditional social and political forms. Bilateral kinship is in some places replaced by corporate patrilineages; men's associations sometimes override kinship relations as decision-making bodies; there are large permanent settlements in some areas; and there are vast differences in types of leadership, from virtual chiefdoms to a virtual absence of authority beyond the head of the family. Some of this variation is undoubtedly secondary, deriving from long contact with agents of Western civilization, such as explorers, whaling crews, traders, and missionaries. However, such diversity does suggest that the hunting-gathering adaptation may permit a wider range of socio-political variation than is accounted for in present typologies (Damas 1968).

Tribes

"If I had to select one word in the vocabulary of anthropology as the single most egregious case of meaninglessness," wrote Morton Fried

(1967:154), "I would have to pass over 'tribe' in favor of 'race.' " The comparison is apt; like "race," the concept of "tribe" is used to refer to a vast range of entities which have almost nothing in common with each other.

There are three basic objections to the concept of "tribe": (1) it does not encompass a discrete group of societies that share common qualities; (2) it is not sufficiently different from other types, such as bands and chiefdoms; (3) it suggests a degree of social integration, or at least boundedness, that is often nonexistent (Helm 1968).

Why, then, is the term in use at all? There are both logical and empirical reasons. First, the term is a recognition that both in sociopolitical complexity and in evolutionary development there *must* be a form that bridges the gap between hunting-gathering bands and centralized systems. Second, cross-cultural studies do reveal features in common to at least many of these groups.

Tribes are uncentralized egalitarian systems in which authority is distributed among a number of small groups; unity of the larger society is established from a web of individual and group relations. Because these groups rely on domesticated food sources, they are more densely populated and usually more sedentary than hunting-gathering bands. As with bands, there is little political or economic specialization, except for a division of labor along age and sex lines, and there is no religious professionalization. However, according to Elman Service (1962), the defining quality of the tribe—that which separates it from the band—is the existence of "pan-tribal sodalities" which unite the various self-sufficient communities into wider social groups. A "sodality" is simply a formal or informal association, such as a family group, a college fraternity, or the Boy Scouts. In tribal societies there are two types of sodalities: those which are derived from kinship, and those which are not. Kinship sodalities include lineages—groups tracing descent through either the male line (patrilineage) or the female line (matrilineage)—and clans, which are groups of lineages tracing common descent to an often-mythical ancestor. Non-kin sodalities include a host of voluntary and involuntary associations.

If we look at tribes in terms of the types of sodalities that unite them, or in terms of who makes the decisions for the group, we find that a number of subtypes immediately emerge. Even where other forms of sodalities are evident, kinship will almost invariably be an important element of social integration. One form of political organization based on kinship is the *segmentary lineage*, especially common in Africa, in which a number of autonomous village groups can join together in ever-larger units for ritual purposes or to counter some threat. Many tribal societies are integrated by *associations* which cross-cut kinship divisions. In "age-set" systems, the group initiated together at puberty will form a continuing sodality that takes on different functions as it passes through certain age levels. For example (if the group is male) as young men they will form a warrior society, and as elders they will become the governing body of the community. In other tribes, such as the American Plains Indians, voluntary societies of warriors, "clowns," or "police" may serve important integrating and decision-making functions. While tribal societies do not have hierarchies of full-time religious professionals, religion may be extremely important, especially if it is tied to some sort of ancestor veneration, as is often the case in unilineal groups. In these societies, *ritual stratification* may be a key element of integration as those responsible for major rituals assume decision-making leadership even in secular matters. In some tribes, *village councils of elders* will make public decisions, usually through a process of discussion leading to consensus. Finally, throughout Melanesia certain *"big men"* attain significant political authority through wealth, generosity, and courage in war. While these leaders may exercise chieftain-like authority, their position is inherently unstable, since it is dependent on their ability to buy followers through gift-giving and loans. A bad crop, an inability to gather sufficient pigs for a lavish feast, or failure in battle can quickly shift authority to a contender with better luck.

It is tempting to think of such a breakdown of subtypes as fairly covering the range of possibilities, but there are tribes that include elements from more than one subtype, and others that do not fit any of these forms. Why this endless profusion of subtypes? Perhaps the basic problem is in attempting to define "tribe" in political terms at all. Unlike "band," "chiefdom," and "state," the concept of "tribe" really does not—and cannot—refer to a particular type of political organization, since there seem to be few structural, or systemic, limits on the variety of forms. Ronald Cohen's characterization of this midrange group of societies as noncentralized "polities based on domesticated plants and animals" might be the best we can do and still allow for the range of variation. Even here, we are faced with certain rather glaring anomalies. The American Plains Indians, some of whom lacked domesticated plants or food animals (their subsistence was almost entirely based on the buffalo), certainly had more complex integrating institutions than those found in hunting-gathering bands.

THE KPELLE. Just how complex all this can get is illustrated by the Kpelle of West Africa. Here, the larger cultural group is fragmented into a number of self-sufficient communities, each with a hereditary "owner of the land" but also with a council of elders that makes decisions by consensus. Complementing the political power of these groups is the men's secret society (secret in the sense that its symbols and rituals are not to be revealed to outsiders). This society, the Poro, holds a super-natural political power that cuts across lineage and small chiefdom bound-aries and can thus unite the Kpelle into larger groups. Actually, the Poro extends far beyond the Kpelle, including a host of cultures in Nigeria, the Ivory Coast, Liberia, Sierra Leone, Ghana, and Portuguese Guinea. In the past it arbitrated in local wars and even united entire countries for common action in times of emergency. Thus we find the centralization and hierarchy we expect from chiefdoms, the segmentary organization and pantribal sodalities common to tribes, and at least three of our sub-types—"associational," "village council," and "ritually stratified"—com-bined in the Kpelle (Fulton 1972; Little 1965).

THE YANOMAMO. The Yanomamo are a horticultural group living in scattered villages in Venezuela and northern Brazil. As described by Napoleon Chagnon (1968), these people are extremely aggressive and war-like. Their self-conscious fierceness derives from a vicious circle in which a premium on male warrior qualities justifies extensive female infanticide, with the result that there is a severe shortage of women. As men must go to war to capture wives, they have come to place a high value on masculine warlike qualities. The constant aggression of the Yanomamo creates a number of political problems both within the village and be-tween villages. Polygamy, mainly reserved for the older and wealthier men, exacerbates the shortage of women. Also, there is a marriage rule which gives older brothers first right for brides, and a broad definition of incest that further reduces the women available to younger men. The result is that within villages brothers are pitted against brothers, adultery and accusations of adultery are common, and hostility levels are high. The maintenance of order in such a situation would seem to demand a strong headman, but, as with bands, the headman has no coercive au-thority. Within the village, the men are kept from killing each other by a system of conventionalized violence: taking turns hitting each other with the fist on the side or chest, or striking each other on the head with long poles. The political leader's function in these battles is to maintain the level of violence within the rules, that is, just this side of lethal.

Intervillage politics is a matter of survival. Unlike many horticultural tribes that participate in warfare almost as a game, the Yanomamo are deadly serious; it is not unknown for entire villages to be overrun, with all the men killed or dispersed and all the women taken captive. In order to maintain a balance of power, a village must often form alliances with former enemies. This takes place in three stages: first, ritual exchange of goods; second, mutual feasting; and finally, exchange of women as wives. Nevertheless, alliances are tenuous, and may be broken with impunity, especially in the early stages.

In many ways, the Yanomamo would seem a typical tribe: their social organization is certainly more complex than that of nomadic hunters and gatherers; their villages are permanent and relatively stable (they tend to fission after reaching a certain size); yet, there is no centralized coercive leadership and there is equal access to headmanship positions among the men of the village. However, these otherwise obviously "tribal" people seem to lack the one thing Service held to be the defining quality of tribes, namely, pantribal sodalities. It is true that lineages extend beyond village boundaries, but they do not unite villages; not, at least, in the absence of military alliances. In fact, because of the hostilities created within lineages through competition over women, bonds of marriage are often stronger than patrilineal bonds. There are no pantribal associations, and military alliances unite only two or a few villages. Certainly no political structure integrates the entire Yanomamo group or even a large proportion of it.

THE NUER.   The Nuer of southern Sudan, described by E.E. Evans-Pritchard in 1940, provide a classic example of the "segmentary lineage" solution to the problem of tribal unity. About 200,000 Nuer live in villages, cultivating maize and millet during the rainy season, herding cattle in almost constant nomadism during the dry season. Their social system is fluid in the extreme, and individually they have a reputation for being fiercely independent. While they completely lack centralized authority, or any formal authority at all beyond the village level, they have been able to join together in large groups to counter external threat. Evans-Pritchard characterizes the Nuer as "an acephalous state, lacking legislative, judicial, and executive organs. Nevertheless, it is far from chaotic. It has a persistent and coherent form which might be called 'ordered anarchy.'"

The smallest corporate economic unit is the household, comprised of several patrilineally-related men and their families. A group of these households may be clustered as a "hamlet" within a village. As one of these hamlets grows through processes of birth, adoption, and immigration, it will inevitably fission, creating another group which may form a hamlet in a nearby village. These hamlets will make up a minor lineage, and several of them, spread between many villages, will make up larger and larger units: major lineage, maximal lineage, and finally, clan. A clan might include thousands of people and be spread throughout all Nuerland, creating a network of social ties which these highly mobile people can call upon as needed. Since clans are exogamous, marriage alliances establish hundreds of small bonds with other clans.

Parallel to the segmentary lineage system, but not identical with it, is a territorial system. Each clan "owns" a certain territory which is, however, open to members of other clans; in fact, the "owner" clan does not form an aristocracy and may actually populate only a small portion of its territory. However, those moving into a village will attempt to establish relations with an owner lineage through being adopted into it or through marriage.

War and feuding are almost constant. By means of a process of "complementary opposition," increasingly larger territorial groups can be united for such purposes. For example, two sections may be fighting with each other, but they will ally if another group attacks both. To counter an even larger threat, all three former antagonists may join together. The political unity of the Nuer must be defined situationally as increasingly larger units are assembled according to need, and then dismantled when the threat is gone.

The "complementary opposition" solution to the problem of tribal integration, shown in Figure 3, is especially adaptive for a tribe that intrudes into an already occupied territory. This is the case with the Nuer, who have within historical times expanded into the land of the Dinka. Such a system, extremely flexible yet capable of forming a powerful united force, channels expansion outward and releases internal pressures in warfare against other peoples (Sahlins 1961).

Centralized Systems

As noted previously, a valid typology should designate *systems*, so that within any single category the determination of one or a few variables will predict others. The category "centralized political systems" encompasses societies in which power and authority inhere in one person or group of persons. This is true by definition—that is tautological. But by extension we can predict that these societies will tend to be more densely populated than bands and tribes, will be stratified by rank or class, will have specialized social and occupational roles, will utilize more productive technology, will have economies based on centralized redistribution, and will be more stable in terms of ongoing sociopolitical groupings. Morton Fried emphasizes the basic inequalities of these systems relative to uncentralized systems: recruitment into political positions is no longer equal but may be based on membership in a certain class or in an elite lineage.

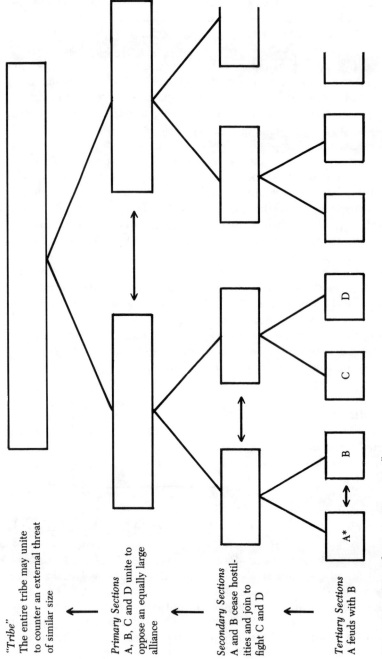

"Tribe"
The entire tribe may unite
to counter an external threat
of similar size

Primary Sections
A, B, C and D unite to
oppose an equally large
alliance

Secondary Sections
A and B cease hostil-
ities and join to
fight C and D

Tertiary Sections
A feuds with B

A*   B   C   D

Fig. 3 Nuer "Complementary Opposition"

*Each box in the bottom row represents several allied villages.

Though unilineal descent groups may exist, and even hold a great deal of local power, politics is no longer manifested mainly through kinship; political specialization appears with full-time politicians and an attendant bureaucracy.

Chiefdoms

In respect to social integration, the chiefdom level transcends the tribal level in two major ways: (1) it has a higher population density made possible by more efficient productivity, and (2) it is more complex, with some form of centralized authority. Unlike segmentary systems, in which political units coalesce and dissolve according to the situation, chiefdoms have relatively permanent central agencies of government, typically based on collection and redistribution of an economic surplus (often including a labor surplus).

The position of chief, unlike that of headman of a band or lineage, is a position of at least minimal "power"—that is, the chief has access to a certain amount of coercion. The chief may be the final authority in the distribution of land, and may be able to recruit an army. Economically, he is the center and coordinator of the redistribution system: he can collect taxes of food or goods, some of which will be returned to the populace, creating a new level of group solidarity in which a number of specialized parts depend on the smooth functioning of the whole (Durkheim's "organic solidarity"). Even if the chief's position is not directly hereditary, it will only be available to certain families or lineages. While actual class stratification is absent, every individual is ranked according to membership in a descent group; those closer to the chief's lineage will be higher on the scale and receive the deference of all those below. Indeed, according to Service (1971:145), "the most distinctive characteristic of chiefdoms, as compared to tribes and bands, is . . . the pervasive inequality of persons and groups in the society."

However, the chief by no means possesses absolute power. The aristocratic ethos does not carry with it any formal, legal apparatus of forceful repression, and what obedience the chief can command may derive less from fear of physical sanctions than from his direct control of the economic redistributional system. The chief's lineage may itself become exceptionally wealthy, but ultimately loyalty is purchased by constant bestowal of goods and benefits. Though there may be the approximation of a bureaucracy, offices beneath that of chief are not clearly differentiated, and when pressures build up these lower bureaucrats can break away from the parent body and set up an opposition government. Thus a chief is in some ways comparable to a Latin American *caudillo*, in the sense that he walks a narrow tightrope between conflicting interest groups and maintains his position through a precarious balancing act.

Though definitions of "tribe" have often been accused of being so general as to be meaningless, the above description of the "chiefdom" level of political integration—derived largely from Elman Service (1971)—has been accused of being too specific. According to Herbert Lewis (1968), Service has logically deduced this model according to what *should* exist between the tribal and state levels, then joined it with the specific model of Polynesian political structure, and proposed this hybrid as a general evolutionary type. Lewis points out that many groups which appear to have chieftainships are not stable at all; they oscillate back and forth from centralized leadership to egalitarianism as strong leaders come and go. But by this time, such looseness in our categories should be assumed without another long disclaimer.

PRECOLONIAL HAWAII. The eight islands of aboriginal Hawaii were under the domination of a number of rigidly stratified hereditary chiefdoms. The paramount chiefs were believed to be descendants of the gods and were so charged with *mana*—supernatural power—that even the ground they walked on could not be touched by lesser mortals. The chiefly personage was thus surrounded by an elaborate set of taboos, the breaking of which could mean a sentence of death. The chiefs were supreme economic, military, and ritual leaders, though most of these functions were delegated to a group of noble administrators and war leaders who formed the upper strata of society. There were two other levels below these administrators: lesser nobles and commoners. Each individual belonged to one of these strata, and the nobles were also ranked according to the order of their birth and their nearness to the high chief. The higher nobles, or lesser chiefs, were accorded a great deal of deference; for example, commoners had to throw themselves face down on the ground as they passed. In order to keep the chiefly line pure, the heir to the position of high chief was supposed to be the first-born son of the chief and his firstborn sister (a form of incestuous endogamy we also find in ancient Egypt and Inca Peru).

Lesser chiefs controlled allocations of land and water—the latter exceedingly important, since much of the productive land was irrigated. They also, de facto, controlled the communal labor of commoners. Tribute was paid to the high chief by the upper level nobles, who collected from the lower nobles, and so on down the line to the commoners. This tribute—or some of it—would be used in public works, mainly irrigation canals and warfare. Nobles also subsidized a group of professional crafts-men from the tribute till.

What kept these polities from attaining the status of "states" was par-tially the lack of differentiation of the political sphere; these were he-reditary theocracies in which authority was still relatively undifferentiated from religion and kinship. Also, though a chief might hold life and death power over his subjects in some regards, the central governing unit by no means held a monopoly on this power, which was distributed among a number of lesser chiefs. Nor was there any legal structure to administer such force. Finally, these governments were far from stable. Warfare was constant, and chiefdoms were regularly overthrown, in which case the entire noble class would be replaced by the conquering group (Davenport 1967; Service 1975; Seaton 1978).

THE KWAKIUTL. Indian societies of the Northwest Coast of North America are usually categorized as chiefdoms, though these groups do not fit the ideal pattern as neatly as do the Hawaiians.

The Kwakiutl Indians of Vancouver Island were never studied in their aboriginal state; by the time Franz Boas began his fieldwork among them in 1885, they had already had almost a century of contact with white traders, missionaries, sailors, and Indian agents, and had been decimated by disease. At that time their plane of living, based on hunting and fishing and virtually devoid of domesticated food supplies, was among the highest in North America as measured by material possessions—houses, canoes, utensils, tools, and such "art" objects as totem poles.

The Kwakiutl were divided into about 25 villages, each of which was comprised of from two to seven *numayma*, or tightly cohesive units made up of from one to several extended families. *Numayma* were stratified in terms of prestige within the village, and each individual was ranked within his *numayma*. Ranks, which were obtained mainly through heredity or marriage, were intricately elaborated by titles, crests and ceremonial privileges.

Such prestige positions were by no means rare; out of a population of about 1,500 individuals, there were 650 named positions, some of which were held by more than one person at the same time. These social positions were maintained through the medium of the *potlatch*—an elab-orate feast in which an enormous amount of goods were distributed to all present. One could also insult a rival by destroying goods in his presence, but these rivalry potlatches, though dramatic, were not as common as is often believed.

The Kwakiutl obviously suggest many elements of the classical chiefdom: a strong system of ranking, specialized leadership roles based on heredity, permanent agencies of government, and redistribution. But the fit is far from perfect. First, there was no integration beyond the village, and precious little within it, since most political integration was focused in the *numayma*. The highest ranking chief in the village would supposedly have some extra authority, but in practice the *numayma* were the day-to-day political entity, which means that politics was manifested through kinship, as in tribal society. Also, it is debatable that the potlatch really represented a system of redistribution. No one in Kwakiutl society was sufficiently wealthy to give a potlatch without both calling in debts and borrowing. The potlatch was the center of a complex economic system based on an intricate web of loaner-debtor relationships. Though an invited *numayma* might not be directly involved in such debts, it was expected to reciprocate the potlatch, preferably with greater abundance. Also, the main article distributed at a potlatch was the Hudson Bay blanket, which could hardly be eaten and so was most valuable as a sort of currency used for further loaning and borrowing. Thus the potlatch suggests a system of reciprocity, common to bands and tribes, not the centralized redistribution that is supposedly a defining quality of chiefdoms. In other words, the Kwakiutl, and perhaps all the cultures of the Northwest Coast, would seem to represent a blending of elements of both tribes and chiefdoms (Codere 1950, 1957; Drucker & Heizer 1967).

The State

For Elman Service (1971:163), the distinguishing quality of the state, that which separates it from the chiefdom, "is the presence of that special form of control, the consistent threat of force by a body of persons legitimately constituted to use it." Morton Fried (1967), on the other hand, emphasizes stratification: the state has special institutions, both formal and informal, to maintain a hierarchy with differential access to resources. This stratification goes beyond the individual and lineage ranking found in less complex societies; it involves the establishment of true classes. For Ronald Cohen (1978a, 1978b), the "key diagnostic feature" of the state is its permanence. Unlike lower order forms of political organization, the state does not regularly fission (that is, break up into a number of smaller groups) as part of its normal process of political activity.

States are generally large, complex societies, encompassing a variety of classes, associations, and occupational groups. Occupational specialization, including a full-time political bureaucracy, unites the entire group in a web of interrelated dependencies. Because of the vast range of individual and class interests within a state, pressures and conflicts unknown in less complex societies necessitate some sort of rule of impersonal law, backed by physical sanctions, for the ongoing maintenance of the system.

THE PRECOLONIAL ZULU. The Nguni family of Bantu-speaking peoples included about 100,000 pastoralists and shifting cultivators living in about 80,000 square miles of southeastern Africa. The basic residence unit was the patrilineally extended family. The largest permanent political unit was the clan, though several clans might temporarily form a "tribe." Actually, these were classic chiefdoms, as described above.

During the early years of the nineteenth century, most of these independent chiefdoms were united through conquest into the powerful and highly militaristic Zulu state. To a great extent, this relatively undeveloped state owed its continuing unity to the threat of the Boers and British who were pushing at the edges of its territory (the British conquered the Zulu in 1887). Regiments of conscripted soldiers, belonging to the king alone, were stationed in barracks concentrated in the capital. The king not only had the power to command military and labor service, but also collected "gifts" from his subjects, which made him the wealthiest man in the kingdom. In turn, he was expected to be generous in providing food and other goods for his people. He had a council of advisors whose recommendations, ideally, were followed. He was also the ultimate appeals court for cases referred from the lower chiefs' courts, and he reserved to himself the right of passing death sentences (though the chiefs did not always respect this reservation). Individuals and clans were stratified according to their geneological closeness to the king.

Thus, though inchoate and short-lived, the Zulu state displayed many of the attributes of more complex states: it united a large number of disparate groups under a central authority; it claimed, at least in theory, a monopoly on the use of force; its power was allocated through a complex bureaucracy; and it maintained government by objective law.

However, much of the old chiefdom stage remained—so much that the people themselves seemed to think of the state as a glorified chiefdom. The state was essentially a collection of clans which were still relatively independent. Loyalties were inevitably divided between chief and king, with the people often siding with the local group. Chiefs retained day-to-day rules, including the right to use force to put down rebellions, as long as the king was informed. The idea persisted that a bad king could be overthrown, just as a bad chief could, as long as the individual and not the system was changed; in fact, kingly succession was largely a matter of assassination or rebellion. Also, while there was definite social stratification, it was much the same as that of the Hawaiians (individuals and clans ranked according to their geneological closeness to the king). Nor was occupational specialization much more developed than in the prestate period. In short, while definitely a state in regard to unification of a number of formerly autonomous groups under centralized government, the precolonial Zulu encompassed many of the aspects of the chiefdoms upon which it was based (Gluckman 1940; Service 1975).

THE INCA. At the beginning of the fifteenth century, a powerful chiefdom in the Cuzco Valley of Peru began the military expansion that would create the largest of the pre-Columbian New World states. At its climax, the Inca empire extended 2,700 miles from Central Chile to the present-day border of Ecuador and Colombia, an area that was united without the use of animal transportation (though llamas and alpacas were used as cargo carriers). Contemporary characterizations of the Inca as "communist," "socialist," or a "welfare state" do little justice to this unique adaptation to the ecological, social, and historical conditions of the Andes.

The Inca empire was integrated as much by a system of economic redistributions as by military force or political centralization. Food production was greatly expanded, not through technological innovation but through the increasingly efficient organization of labor—in agricultural terracing, for example, or in constructing extensive irrigation systems—and through transferring entire communities to formerly underutilized areas. Throughout the empire, land was divided in thirds to provide for the common people, the state religion, and the secular bureaucracy. After 1475, there was increasing state ownership, especially of lands newly developed for cultivation or pasture.

Three bureaucracies were supported by this economy. At the top was the central bureaucracy, comprised of ethnic Inca nobles and others who had attained the status of Inca through their contribution to the state. This Cuzco-based bureaucracy consisted of a Royal Court (made up of eleven minor lineages, each with its own palace), a royal advisory council, and more or less specialized agencies to administer the judiciary, the military, education, transportation, and communications. A parallel, and to some degree separate, religious bureaucracy administered a state religion that was fairly "open" in the sense that it was quite capable of incorporating the gods, idols and rituals of the conquered tribes. As much as one-third of the Inca's entire gross national product was devoted to religious ceremony. Finally, a provincial bureaucracy encompassed about 80 regional groups through a hierarchy of local chiefs called *curacas*.

The existence of such sophisticated bureaucratic structures might give the impression that the Inca state had completely overridden and replaced earlier forms of social organization. Yet over millenia, and through the myriad risings and fallings of civilizations, the basic unit of Andean social structure remained the *ayllu*, a lineage-based community in which land was held in common and redistributed according to need. The *ayllu* was highly self-sufficient, unified by common territory and by complex interrelationships of social and economic reciprocity. Each *ayllu* had its own leader, who lacked coercive authority. The *ayllu* cared for its own infirm and aged and achieved public building and maintenance goals through cooperative labor. Many *ayllus* were united into larger tribes and confederacies for trade and defense.

Conquest by the Inca left this fundamental social structure intact, and many state governmental forms and practices were based on those of the *ayllu*. For example, the system of conscripted labor by which the Inca built their phenomenal roads (one road was almost 2,000 miles long), public buildings, and agricultural terraces was a direct extension of traditional *ayllu* collective labor patterns. Even at the highest levels of government the *ayllu* form was the model: each new Inca emperor began a new royal *ayllu* consisting of all his male descendants. According to John Murra, the widespread belief that the Inca polity was divided into groups based on a decimal system is but a literal reading of a census taker's shorthand (records were kept on knotted ropes); the actual division of the empire was the traditional one of *ayllu*, tribe and confederacy. Thus, despite its complexity, the Inca state does not represent a quantum leap in social organization, except in sheer magnitude; rather, it was a drawing together of a number of intact traditional units (Mason 1957; Murra 1958; Shaedel 1978).

The *ayllu*, it might be noted, has already survived the Incas by four centuries, has survived Spanish colonialism, republicanism, and a myriad of dictatorships, and continues to exist intact in many areas of Peru and Bolivia. Today the *ayllu* shows signs of succumbing, finally, not to political pressures or conquest, but to the effects of overpopulation and industrialization (Lewellen 1978).

The value of a typology depends as much on what we want to do with it as on the criteria used in forming it. The classification suggested in this chapter is quite general. However, it is necessary to have some means of developing evolutionary sequences and establishing a standardized vocabulary. Specialists—in peasant politics, for example—will require more precise classification, and may develop any number of subtypes. The specialist in a single culture area, such as the Arctic, might focus on the *variety* of adaptive strategies and thus be fully justified in rejecting any typology at all.

This seems rather obvious, but many of the objections to classification of political systems derive from unsuccessful attempts to directly correlate specific-level data with general-level categories. Criticism should be at the level of the typology itself, that is, at the level of broad cross-cultural statistical probabilities. The crucial question is: What elements of these societies appear together with sufficient regularity for us to consider them integrated parts of the same system? This is an empirical question, and as it is answered with increasing precision we may expect a corresponding increase in the refinement of our classifications.

SUGGESTED READINGS

Cohen, Ronald, and John Middleton (eds.)
Comparative Political Systems (Austin: University of Texas Press, 1967)
Though this anthology seems random in its selection, it does provide studies of a wide range of political types. Among those groups represented are the !Kung, Eskimo, Nambikara, Mapuche, and Inca. The list of authors of these twenty articles reads like a *Who's Who* of cultural anthropology: Claude Lévi-Strauss, Robert Lowie, John Murra, F.G. Bailey, and S.N. Eisenstadt, among others.

Fried, Morton
The Evolution of Political Society (New York: Random House, 1967)
Fried classifies political systems in terms of an individual's access to power. This gives him the basic categories of "egalitarian," "rank," and "stratified," each of which is described in detail.

Levinson, David, and Martin J. Malone
Toward Explaining Human Culture (New York: HRAF Press, 1980)
This is an admirable attempt to collect in a single short volume much that has been learned about cross-cultural regularities from statistical studies using the Human Relations Area Files. Many of the chapters are valuable in providing quantitative data to support or refute speculation on the classification of political systems.

Service, Elman R.
Primitive Social Organization: An Evolutionary Perspective (New York: Random House, 1962)
This is the book that established "band," "tribe," "chiefdom," and "state" as the basic "levels of sociocultural integration." Despite its subtitle, the book is largely descriptive and makes little attempt at suggesting causes of evolutionary change.

Ancient Egypt is one of the world's six primary states, i.e., those that developed uninfluenced by previously existing states (Library of Congress).

CHAPTER 3

The Evolution of the State

About 5,500 years ago, on the fertile floodplains of the Tigris and Eu-
phrates Rivers in what is today Iraq, there developed a type of society
unique to its time. After millenia in which man had gradually turned
from migratory foraging toward seasonal settlements based on a few domesticated plants and animals, and then toward year-round farming villages, there came into being the world's first true cities, and with them
a novel form of political organization. Previously, society had been structured according to kinship networks; now there appeared a permanent
administrative bureaucracy that demanded loyalties transcending lineage
and clan. Local chiefs relinquished much of their authority to a ruling
class who had the power to gather the agricultural surpluses and call forth
the labor necessary to create large-scale irrigation projects and monu-
mental architecture. Fortified cities, such as Uruk and Ur, boasted populations of upwards of 40,000 "citizens." A full-time caste of priests
presided over a complex temple religion. Craft specialists manufactured
the obsidian knives and gold and silver figurines that would tie vast areas
together through webs of trade. The "state" had been born.

Today, when national populations are counted in the hundreds of millions and power is so concentrated that the word of a president or a
premier could unleash a holocaust of unthinkable proportions, it may be
difficult to realize the significance of the thirteen or so small city-states

collectively known as Sumeria. Just as we can legitimately speak of an "agriculture revolution" or an "industrial revolution" to suggest quantum changes in human social complexity, so can we speak of a "state revolution." Various authorities might argue the defining characteristics of the early state, but none would demean its importance; for here was a new kind of society—a seed bearing the genetic code for the giant nation-states of the modern world.

The Mesopotamian state developed through a long series of adjustments to a particular environment and a specific set of social problems. In retrospect, however, the process seems almost inevitable, for we find similar adaptations leading to similar socio-political structures in Egypt, in the Indus River Valley of India and the Yellow River Valley of northern China, in Mesoamerica, and in Peru. The "primary" states are illustrated in Figure 4. Though these six states appeared hundreds or even thousands of years apart (see Table 2), and though there was minimal commerce between a few of them (such as India and Mesopotamia), each seems to have originated quite independently of the others. This poses a problem: if the state evolved autonomously not once but six times, can we discover fundamental processes that were common to all?

Though far removed from the state, the rudiments of human social evolution can be found in man's closest animal relatives. Among higher primates characterized by marked sexual dimorphism (differences in size and musculature between sexes), such as baboons and gorillas, we find strong male dominance, specialization for defense, and various patterns of ongoing family organization. Some primate species reveal extremely complex elaborations of social structure. Cynocephalus baboons, for example, live in stable groups of forty to eighty individuals, and these bands exhibit clear hierarchies of status and considerable specialization of function among both males and females. Hamadryas baboons forage in small one-male groups but join together in troops of several hundred for sleeping. Some primates pass on significant learned skills from generation to generation and reveal remarkable cooperation in rearing the young, collective defense, grooming, and sexual behavior. However, only the genus *Homo* has extended such basic primate adaptations by cultural means. The most significant of these are *symbolism*, through which man communicates and embellishes both individual and group ideation; and *sharing* (reciprocity), which underlies the division of labor, creates the potential for increasingly elaborate social organization, and ties kinship groups together through the exchange of wives.

More than 99 percent of man's two- to three-million-year sojourn on Earth has been spent in small bands—flexible, egalitarian, nomadic groups comprised of several extended families. Since contemporary hunt-

Fig. 4 Primary States

Table 2 Chronology of Primary State Development

	Old World				New World	
	Mesopotamia	*Nile Valley, Egypt*	*Indus River Valley, India*	*Yellow River Valley, China*	*Mesoamerica*	*Peru*
1000					Teotehuacán · · Maya	
AD BC			Alexander the Great	Chow Dynasty	Olmec	Chavín · Tiahuanaco · Nazca
1000	Akkadian Empire	New Kingdom		Shang Dynasty	La Venta	Chavín de Huantar
2000	Sumaria (13+ City - States) · Akkad	Middle Kingdom	Indus State	Cheng-Chou An-Yang	San Lorenzo	
3000	Ur	Old Kingdom · Political Unification	Harrapa Mohenjo-Daro			Coastal settlements
4000	Uruk	Early agriculture		Yang-shao culture		
5000	Early agricultural settlements					
6000	Intensive agriculture		Agriculture to 7000 BC	Early farming?	Domestication of corn?	

SOURCES: Claessen 1978; Fagan 1978; Jolly and Plog 1979; Pfeiffer 1977; Wenke 1980.

ing-gathering peoples occupy only the most marginal environments, we should be careful about generalizing their social organization to our remote ancestors, who lived in more hospitable places and climes. Yet archeological evidence from Paleolithic times suggests little elaboration on the basic band form. One reason that this structure may have persisted for so long is that it was an evolutionary dead end. The hunting-foraging adaptation (the Pygmies and traditional Eskimo are contemporary examples) requires an almost perfect ecological balance, in which populations must be maintained below the food supply; thus, there would have been little selective pressure for change. What requires explanation is not why such an excellent adaptation should have lasted so long, but rather why a few groups of people—very few, at first—abandoned it for more complex forms of subsistence and society.

Radically new types of social structure appeared only with the sedentary life styles and greater population densities brought about by the domestication of plants and animals. It should not be supposed, however, that this "revolution" was sudden, or that it immediately led to the formation of the state. Agriculture and animal husbandry apparently developed independently in a number of areas throughout the world, but only a few of these went on to evolve states. In the Tehuacán Valley of Mexico, the period of development from hunting-gathering bands to agriculturally-based states was more than 7,000 years (Flannery 1968). In other areas of primary-state development, too, centralization of government was long preceded by sedentary agriculture, permanent villages, and even extensive irrigation works.

American and Dutch anthropologists have tackled the problem of the origin of the state with enthusiasm (the British and French tend to ignore evolutionary questions). Until recently, such theorists carefully distinguished the six primary states from secondary states, which developed out of or through contact with already existing states. Since virtually all theories focused on the former, evidence was by definition exclusively archeological. Today, some researchers have abandoned the primary-secondary distinction for a typology that allows the inclusion of even recent states, such as the Ankole of Uganda, as long as they remained pristine. We will examine some of this important research later, but first we must look at the "classical" theories of state origins.

Internal Conflict Theories

The doctrine that the state evolved through class struggle is implicit in many of the writings of Karl Marx. However, these ideas were not fully worked out until Frederick Engels's major work, *The Origin of the Family, Private Property and the State* (1891), which was published after his mentor's death. According to Engels, who borrowed heavily from American evolutionary anthropologist Lewis Henry Morgan, the earliest form of social organization was communistic: resources were shared equally by all, and there was no strong concept of personal possession. Technological innovation gives rise to surplus, which allows a class of non-producers to develop. Private ownership is simply a concomitant of commodity production. Once established, private property stimulates an inexorable chain of cause-and-effect that leads to an entrepreneurial class—owners of the means to production and buyers and sellers of human labor. This, in turn, results in differential access to resources, and thus to vast discrepancies in individual wealth. In order to protect its interests against the masses of active producers (who understandably want to share in their own production), the elite must erect a structure of permanent centralized force to protect its class interests.

Given its time, this analysis is sophisticated and subtle. We find in it the perception that the primary means of economic exchange in band and tribal society is reciprocity, and that more complex systems involve concentrations of wealth and redistribution through a central agency, be it chief, king, or bureaucracy. Engels artfully applies Marxian materialism to long-term social evolution; the basic causes of change are held to be technological and economic, not ideational. Also, we find here a clear recognition that social stratification is one of the defining qualities of the state.

Unfortunately, as Elman Service (1975:283) has observed, "there is absolutely no evidence in the early archaic civilizations themselves, nor in archeologically- or historically-known chiefdoms and primitive states, of any important private dealings—i.e., evidence of capitalism." Indeed, the very concepts of "communism" and "capitalism" seem absurd when projected onto band and chiefdom societies, so different from modern industrial states.

Contemporary theorist Morton Fried (1967), who bases his evolutionary typology of political systems on the degree of individual access to resources and positions of prestige, offers a variation on the class-conflict model. Once true stratification exists, Fried notes, the state is already implicit because the maintenance of a class system requires that power be concentrated in the hands of an elite. By its very nature, this creates conflict within the society. Differential access to resources, and the exploitation of human labor, create pressures which are quite unknown in less complex societies. Conflict arising out of social stratification should not be thought of as the cause of state formation; rather, such conflict is merely a prior condition for the development of the state. Incipient social stratification is so unstable that a society which finds itself at such a stage must either disintegrate to a lower level of organization or continue its process of centralizing political power. In other words, once classes begin to separate themselves from hierarchies based on individual or kinship status, power must be fairly rapidly assumed by the privileged elite if the true state is to come into existence.

External Conflict Theories

In the Biblical version of social evolution, the development of cities is a direct result of Cain's primordial murder of his brother Abel. This idea, that states are born in blood and war, was given scientific respectability with the development of Social Darwinism in the latter half of the nineteenth century. Herbert Spencer, chief spokesman for the more violent interpretations of evolutionary theory, applied the idea of "survival of the fittest" mainly to individuals, but it took little imagination to extend this concept to societies. The stronger, more militaristic organizations would inevitably prevail over weaker groups, uniting them under a powerful centralized government with a monopoly on the use of force. Militarism alone, even without warfare, would be sufficient; merely the existence of an external threat which required a large standing army could push a loosely structured society in the direction of strong centralized leadership. Implicit or explicit in such theories, of which Spencer's was one of many, is the idea that state government is modeled on military organization in terms of its hierarchical structure and centralized control of physical force.

A nineteenth-century tendency to oversimplify and overgeneralize is evident in these theories, which are based on a gross misunderstanding of physical evolution. Darwin's rather prosaic idea that the mechanism of evolution is differential reproduction (parents with the most surviving offspring pass on more traits) was transliterated into "the law of tooth and fang," with imagery of big tigers devouring little tigers with much sound and fury. When applied to society, such a theory could—and did—provide the philosophical justification ("Law of Nature, you know!") for colonialism, imperialism, monopoly capitalism, and every other form of exploitation.

As we shall see, cross-cultural research does support the hypothesis that war and conquest are important factors in the development of some states, but there are two important objections to the theory that war is the *primary* cause: first, a society can marshal forces only according to available levels of population and organization, so warfare might better be viewed as a function rather than a cause of a given level of social integration; second, warfare among tribes and chiefdoms is more likely to prevent state formation than to cause it, since groups will simply disperse when threatened by a power greater than themselves (Service 1971; Price 1979).

This latter point is a salient consideration in Robert Carniero's (1967, 1970, 1978) theory of "environmental circumscription." Since warfare is virtually universal and usually has the effect of dispersing people rather than uniting them, conflict could only lead to centralization in particular situations. After examining primary-state development in both the Old and New Worlds, Carniero notes that a common denominator is that "they are all areas of circumscribed agricultural land"; that is, they are bounded by mountains, sea, or desert. When there is no such circumscription, population pressures on the environment can be expanded outward, and losers in a war can resettle in a new area. This is not possible where the only arable land is surrounded by unproductive land. Population pressure must then be resolved by unification and by increases in productive capacity—both characteristics of the state—and losers in a war lacking means of escape, must submit to their conquerers. Amazonian Indians waged frequent war for revenge, the taking of women, personal prestige, and the like; but these wars never resulted in widespread conquest by a central power, since new areas of forest could always be found in which to start a new village. However, the riverine valleys of coastal Peru—surrounded by sea, desert, and mountains—offer no such options. As the small, dispersed villages of the Neolithic grew and fissioned, the narrow valleys became increasingly crowded. Intensification of agriculture, through terracing, for example, would only solve the problem temporarily. Revenge warfare would turn to warfare over land, with one group trying to increase its productive capacity at the expense of others. Yet for the weaker in these conflicts, there would be no place to escape that could provide even minimal subsistence; submission to a dominant force was the only viable survival strategy. In this way, a number of independent chiefdoms would be brought under a single hierarchical military government.

Circumscription need not be strictly physical; it can also be social. The Yanomamo of the Venezuelan jungle are not physically circumscribed, but village fission and expansion into virgin territory is easier for those at the periphery of the tribal group than for those near the center. According to Carniero's theory, we would expect that central villages, surrounded by other warring villages, would tend to be larger and have more powerful headmen than peripheral villages, and this is indeed the case. While the Yanomamo are far from the state level of cultural integration, the socially circumscribed villages do exhibit greater tendencies toward centralization.

Carniero subsumes these processes under "the principle of competitive exclusion," derived from evolutionary biology. This principle states that "two species occupying and exploiting the same portion of the habitat cannot coexist indefinitely"—one must ultimately eliminate the other. In applying this idea to societies, Carniero observes that throughout history chiefdoms have been united into states and states have gone to war to create larger states, with competition and selection increasingly tending toward larger and larger units. In plotting the decreasing number of autonomous political units in the world from 1000 B.C., Carniero predicts the political unification of the entire planet by about the year 2300. Assuming, of course, that our leaders do not succumb to a nuclear version of the law of tooth and fang long before then.

"Hydraulic Civilization"

The importance of irrigation to state formation was recognized as early as the writings of Marx and Engels, who noted that a major difference between small-scale agricultural communities and state societies was that the latter required the support of extensive irrigation systems. More recently, Julian Steward (1955) has emphasized irrigation as the fundamental mechanism of state development, since water control permitted sufficient agricultural intensification to create large population densities, and the construction of massive hydraulic systems required new levels of social organization, power, and coordination of labor.

It was Karl Wittfogel (1957) who elaborated the "hydraulic theory" in such detail that his name is now almost exclusively associated with it. Neolithic farmers in the areas of primary-state development, such as Egypt or the riverine valleys of Peru, were dependent on flood irrigation; their fields were watered once a year and new soil was deposited by the annual flood. But flood irrigation is quite variable, and even in the best of times it provides only one crop per year. Slowly, farmers began to exercise control of the floods with dikes and reservoirs, preserving and taming the precious water which could then be released as needed through a network of canals. Early irrigation systems were small and primitive, involving only the labor of a few neighboring farms; but as the productive capacity of the land increased and the human population burgeoned, irrigation works grew in size and complexity. A group of specialists emerged to plan and coordinate the construction of these systems, and later to control the flow of water. This group, whose hands now quite literally held the very life of the community, developed into an administrative elite that governed despotic, centralized states.

This model has fared surprisingly well. Irrigation seems to have been important in all of the primary states. The lowland Maya of the Yucatan Peninsula in Mexico were believed to be an exception until recent aerial photographs revealed that this civilization too was reliant on elaborate irrigation systems. However, the hydraulic theory should not be interpreted in too rigid a cause-and-effect manner: in some areas, for example, complex irrigation systems long preceded state development, while in others (such as Mesopotamia) large-scale water control systems only developed after at least the initial stages of the state. Furthermore, in the American southwest and other areas large hydraulic systems existed for centuries without political centralization. Finally, the theory has only the most tenuous application to secondary states, many of which possessed the most rudimentary irrigation.

These objections may be beside the point. Marvin Harris (1977) has noted that Wittfogel's theory is not really about the origin of the state *per se*, but rather about the development of certain types of managerial systems. To postulate centralization of despotic power around the management of water supplies is not to deny the importance of population density, trade, warfare, environmental circumscription, and other factors which have had key roles in the increasing integration of society.

Population Pressure

From about 23000 B.C. until 2000 A.D., world population will have grown from an estimated 3.5 million to 6.5 billion and from a density of .1 persons per square mile to 124 per square mile (Campbell 1979:462–463). The correlation between this increase in population and the rise of the state has been noted by virtually all evolutionary cultural anthropologists. Robert Carniero (1967) plotted the relation between population density and social complexity in 46 societies and found a significant statistical correspondence between the two variables. Though the correspondence held, at least loosely, for "arithmetic density" (that is, the average number of people per square mile over an entire territory), we find a much stronger relationship if "economic density" alone is considered. Economic density is the relation between population and sources of production. For example, in Egypt the vast majority of people are concentrated in a narrow strip of arable land on either side of the Nile.

According to the early-nineteenth-century economist Thomas Malthus, population is negatively checked by disease, famine, and war as it threatens to outgrow the food supply. However, if this were the only principle operating, population growth would have stabilized at a much lower level than today's. Certainly, one possible response to population pressure on food supply is exactly the opposite of the Malthusian checks; the food supply itself may be increased through some sort of intensification of production, often involving the development of a new technology or the refinement of an existing one. Irrigation, terracing, fertilization, using animal labor, cultivating more types of crops, and exploiting previously unused lands can significantly increase the carrying capacity of a given territory. The resulting increases in population density require more complex forms of social and political organization. This correspondence between population and social evolution was most extensively elaborated by Ester Boserup (1965). In a slight variation on the theory, Michael Harner (1970) argues that population pressure is not only directly responsible for some form of intensification of food production, but also leads to unequal access to resources and subsequently to increasing social stratification.

Marvin Harris, in *Cannibals and Kings* (1977), incorporates these ideas into a complicated "techno-environmental determinist" argument in which social organization and ideology are viewed as the results of a society's technological adaptation to its physical environment. Harris begins by noting the main objection to population pressure theories, namely, that populations usually tend to stabilize comfortably below the carrying capacity of the land. Indeed, all societies have cultural means of supplementing Malthusian checks on population. Hunting-gathering groups maintained relative population equilibrium for tens of thousands of years, and the few such societies which survive today depend on balancing population to food supply. In all preindustrial societies, such practices as female infanticide, two- or three-year-long taboos on sexual intercourse with a woman after she has borne a child, and prolonged nursing (which delays ovulation) serve to keep population in balance with food production. It is only in modern times that population has been allowed to grow unchecked. If population equilibrium was the norm in most premodern societies, we must ask why population might increase to the point where it would force more complex forms of social organization.

Harris's explanation is that during the Pleistocene Era, which lasted until about 10,000 to 15,000 years ago, hunting bands had come to rely on an abundance of large game, and populations had stabilized at levels made possible by such resources. At the end of the Pleistocene hundreds of big game species became extinct, for reasons still not entirely understood, with the result that people had to rely increasingly on alternative sources of food. Wild plants susceptible to domestication had always been available but had been rejected for cost-benefit reasons; without population pressure, hunting and foraging was more expedient for expending a minimum of calories. Now, plant domestication raised the carrying capacity of the land, allowing populations to increase. Population would tend ultimately to stabilize, but over time—perhaps hundreds of years— a gradual and inevitable decrease in productivity occurs as agricultural land loses nutrients and game is overhunted to supply animal protein. In other words, pressure is created not only by population growth, which might be quite slow, but also by a natural decline in the productivity of the land.

In tribal societies, populations are often controlled through a "male supremacist complex" which develops out of constant warfare. A premium on masculine fierceness conversely diminishes the value of women, so that female infanticide—certainly one of the most effective means of population control—becomes virtually normative (some societies have actually institutionalized the killing of the firstborn if it is a female). Agriculturalists have another option: instead of reducing population, they can increase their work-load or add a new technology to augment production. This leads to agricultural surpluses, which are collected and redistributed by "big men" who use their role to gain and maintain status and power. These redistributive chiefs—often war chiefs as well—take on the role of a centralized coercive force. At this point, Harris brings in both Carniero's circumscription theory and Wittfogel's hydraulic theory to show the conditions under which centralization will continue until the state is formed.

It should be noted that to Harris the "initial kick" for this whole process is population; but, in a reverse on the Boserup theory, he sees a relatively stable population adapting to a diminution of food supplies. A major element of the theory—one not too auspicious for the future of civilization—is that any form of productivity will gradually lead to depletions of primary resources, with the result that all societies must sooner or later face the alternative of collapsing or moving to a new level of intensification. Once the domestication of plants and animals becomes the basis for subsistence, there can be no long-term stabilization.

Harris's argument, while appealing, is open to challenge because these processes do not appear to be universal. For example, population pressure on resources cannot, in every area that became politically centralized, be related to decline in productivity. Also, Boserup may be correct in placing her emphasis on population growth rather than resource depletion. Even relatively minor changes in nutrition can radically alter the size of a population. Food supplies are quite elastic and can easily be affected either by a redefinition of usable food resources or by slight changes in technology. As Harris and others have pointed out, population growth may indeed need explaining, but not very much explaining.

The Institutionalization of Leadership

Elman Service, in *Origins of the State and Civilization* (1975), proposes an "integrative" theory. After an extensive review of the rise of the six archaic primary states and a number of modern primitive states, he rejects all conflict theories. Warfare and conquest, he points out, are too universal in human experience to count as causes of a particular form of social organization, and "the only instances we find of permanent subordination from war are where government already exists" (Service 1975:271). Arguments based on irrigation or other forms of intensification admit too many exceptions. In ancient Peru, for example, agricultural intensification was achieved through canal irrigation 1,500 years before the first truly urbanized state. The idea that population pressures create conflicts that can only be solved by centralized government is rejected partially on the grounds that such pressure could just as well lead to increased sharing.

These "negative conclusions" derive from a particular reading of the data; they would hardly be convincing to an ardent proponent of any of the theories rejected. Indeed, while it is conflict theory that is specifically rebutted, implicitly what is being rejected is cultural materialism. What Service has done is to shift the argument from ecological determinants to strategies of decision making.

Service traces a logical development from the basic inequality inherent in human society to formalized and centralized inequality. In all societies, even the most egalitarian bands and tribes, certain individuals stand out by reason of their exceptional talent, intelligence, strength, or beauty. While it is completely natural to confer status upon such people, the resulting inequalities remain individual, rather than class-based, and do not confer privilege or wealth. Certain circumstances tend to favor centralization of effort—for example, when a variety of local ecological niches forces specialization of production and symbiotic trade, or when collaborative work on public projects requires a division of labor. Such circumstances also favor centralized redistribution, which will naturally be handled by the exceptional people of the society (such as the Melanesian "big men," who are usually war chiefs). Because such centralization offers obvious benefits, there will be a snowball effect leading to increasing concentration of administration. This enhancement of leadership, though economic, is not based on ownership, as Engels would have it; rather, it is "the result of a form of dependence that in primitive society results from generosity, from favors given" (Service 1975:293).

Such leadership is unstable because it depends on an individual, who may get sick, die, or simply run out of luck, and there is no formal method of succession. In order for a society to maintain the benefits of centralization, temporary charismatic leadership must be transformed into a permanent hierarchy. When this stage is reached, we have a chiefdom, the first true "institutionalization of power," which is also an institutionalization of inequality. As this power center grows, so does the need of the newly developed ruling class to protect its privilege. One method of doing so, aside from the use of force, is to legitimize the power elite by connecting it with the supernatural, by giving it divine sanction. The use of force, then, far from creating the state, actually represents a temporary failure of the state to function responsibly by providing such benefits as protection, redistribution, and coordination of trade. Thus, "political evolution can be thought to consist, in important part, of 'waging peace' in ever wider contexts" (Service 1975:297).

It should be evident that this is not merely a shift of *emphasis* from population pressure, irrigation, or environmental circumscription, but rather a shift in the *kind* of theory offered. The "considerable exaltation" a leader's successes could produce "in the minds of his followers" (Service 1975:291) would be of little relevance to Robert Carniero or Marvin Harris, who view whole social systems as reacting in survival terms to material environmental determinants. Service's theory shifts the weight of argument from environment to cognition, that is, to the people's perception of accruing benefits. Service also uses models based on cooperation and integration, whereas most other theories have held conflict and instability to be the fundamental conditions out of which the state develops.

Service's point of view is refreshingly innovative. Yet conflict and integration are definitely not mutually exclusive; all societies are involved in both, alternately and simultaneously. Similarly, societies are "materialist" and "cognitive" at the same time. Each perspective offers much in the way of explanation, but to claim exclusivity for one or the other is rather like claiming that a glass of water is half full rather than half empty.

Systems Theories

Few anthropologists today would hold to a single-cause model of the evolution of states (it should be pointed out that those theories regularly referred to as unicausal—Carniero's, Wittfogel's, Boserup's—are really singular only in emphasis). All involve interactions between such factors as population, environment, technology, and irrigation. Synthetic models, like that of Marvin Harris, make these interactions more explicit. However, all such models are based on the idea that, given certain preconditions, particular causes will lead to particular effects in a more or less sequential manner.

Unlike theories which designate specific causes, "systems" models are based on sets of principles, drawn mainly from physics and biology. These include negative and positive feedback, "initial kick," system self-maintenance, and system self-development. Negative feedback is the process by which a stable system minimizes any deviation from equilibrium. For example, in a hunting-gathering society, an increase in birth rate will be balanced by higher infant mortality rates if population threatens to overgrow the food supply. Positive feedback is just the opposite: a small deviation may set in motion a process of increasing change. If the response to population growth is intensified agriculture, the result will be further population growth that will in turn generate more intensification, and so on until some limit is reached. The "initial kick" that stimulates a negative feedback system into a positive feedback system may be very small. Kent Flannery (1968) hypothesizes that in the Tehuacán Valley of Mexico, the processes leading to the development of civilization were set in motion when nomadic foraging bands began to take care of a few edible wild plants. Over generations, this human intervention caused genetic changes that allowed increased dependence on these semi-domesticated foods, and this led to more sedentary lifestyles and larger populations, which in turn increased dependence on domesticates. This chain of events led eventually to the people settling into year-round farming villages. Stable societies are self-maintaining insofar as they are constantly making small adjustments to changes in the physical and social environment. Once positive feedback processes are set in motion, a society becomes self-developing as population growth, agricultural intensification, urbanization, and political centralization feed on one another in constant circular causality. It should be noted that this is almost the exact reversal of the Newtonian principle that every action must have an equal and opposite reaction; with positive feedback, the most minute "initial kick" can, *over the long run, lead to massive change*. It is no longer necessary to explain the state as the effect of some equally momentous cause.

A number of different systems theories of political evolution have been developed. Some of these focus on environment and technology, while others employ a decision-making perspective. Common to all, however, is the idea that societies respond adaptively to many conditions. The goal of explanation, then, is not to pinpoint one or two factors that cause change in all cases, but to specify the processes by which social systems will alter their internal structures in response to selective pressures. As Ronald Cohen (1978b:142) puts it, "The formation of a state is a funnel-like progression of interactions in which a variety of prestate systems, responding to different determinants of change, are forced by otherwise unresolvable conflicts to choose additional and more complex levels of political hierarchy." The opposition between force and benefit theories, between materialist and cognitive paradigms, and between conflict and integration models becomes blurred, since a systems model can incorporate these various perspectives simultaneously.

One such approach has been developed by Clifford Jolly and Fred Plog (1979). In their specific example of the Valley of Mexico, population growth was the initial stimulus, but theoretically any other stimulus which put exceptional stress on the equilibrium system would have been sufficient to cause significant change. Several options were available, given such stress: to reduce the population through infanticide or other cultural means, to disperse the larger settlements, to migrate to new areas, or to intensify agricultural production. Of these alternatives, only the latter would have led to the formation of the state. There are several conditions under which the option for intensification might be chosen: agricultural land might be circumscribed so there would be no place to disperse; farmers could drift into intensification without realizing it, perhaps through a slight new technology like small irrigation canals; or the people might be forced by a conquering group to pay tribute and thus to increase production. In any case, once the option is chosen, it will lead by a series of feedback loops to nucleation, stratification, differentiation, and centralization. Nucleation (roughly synonymous with urbanization) will become necessary for large cooperative labor projects; in turn, as people concentrate in relatively small areas, pressure on local resources will be aggravated, requiring further intensification of food production. Economic stratification develops as more productive farming techniques amplify slight environmental differences, so that a person possessing even marginally better agricultural land will become richer relative to his neighbors. These forces also promote centralization of decision making, since such concentration is more effective for planning large-scale projects and organizing labor. Farming becomes more differentiated as entire fields are turned over to a single crop in order to increase the efficiency of plowing and irrigation. A surplus of food ensures that some do not need to work as farmers at all, and this permits the development of craft specialization. Finally, each one of these factors stimulates the others. The model developed by Jolly and Plog is shown in Figure 5.

It should be noted that this model uses many of the same elements as the so-called "unicausal" and synthetic theories. However, a major difference between this model and that of, say, Marvin Harris is that Jolly and Plog are much less specific about the actual train of events. The processes with which they deal (nucleation, differentiation, etc.) are abstract and can involve stresses deriving from any number of sources. Society is viewed not as a row of dominoes falling in a predictable pattern, but as a flexible, adaptive system making constant internal adjustments to various stresses. These adjustments modify the environment, and this requires further adaptations of the social system in a self-developing process.

The Early State: The Cross-Cultural Evidence

To date, the most extensive attempt to bring together cross-cultural data on state evolution is *The Early State* (1978), edited by Henri J.M. Claessen and Peter Skalník. Unfortunately, this detailed examination of nineteen formative states, ranging from Egypt in 3000 B.C. to the contemporary Kachari of India, completely ignores the distinction between primary and secondary states. This omission is both deliberate and legitimate. So much emphasis has been put on primary-state development that the rich evidence of social evolution provided by other historical states, even those that developed with a great deal of autonomy, has been too often neglected. However, since most of the theories discussed here were originally applied almost exclusively to primary states, it is difficult to appraise Claessen and Skalník's evaluations, based as they are on evidence drawn from a different set of societies.

In any case, this massive work offers a wealth of data and conclusions from a wide range of social systems that fall within the authors' definition of "the early state" as "a centralized socio-political organization for the regulation of social relations in a complex, stratified society divided into at least two basic strata, or emergent social classes—viz. the rulers and the ruled—, whose relations are characterized by political dominance of the former and tributary obligations of the latter, legitimized by a common ideology . . ." (Claessen & Skalník 1978:640). This definition, which summarizes many of the regularities found in the sample, supports the view that class stratification is a primary quality of the state; but it is not necessarily a cause, since differential access to material resources may exist long before the state comes into existence. Indeed, social stratification together with an economy that is capable of producing a surplus

Table 3 Typology of Twenty-One Early States

	Inchoate	Typical	Transitional
Examples (and period covered in sample)	Ankole (Uganda) 1650–1900 A.D. Hawaii 1700–1850 A.D. Norway 900–1100 A.D. Tahiti 1700–1800 A.D. Volta (Upper Volta and Ghana) 1400–1900 A.D. Zande (Sudan) 1750–1850 A.D.	Angkor (Cambodia) 1150–1300 A.D. Axum (Ethiopia) 25–625 B.C. Egypt 2950–2500 B.C. Inca (Peru) 1425–1532 A.D. Kachari (India) 1800 A.D.– Mongolia 1200–1325 A.D. Scythia (Ukrain) 400–725 A.D. Yoruba (Nigeria) 1400–1900 A.D.	Aztecs (Mexico) 1425–1521 A.D. China 250 B.C.–225 A.D. France 900–1100 A.D. Jimma (Ethiopia) 1825 A.D.– Kuba (Zaire) 1850–1900 A.D. Maurya (India) 1100–1275 A.D.
Trade and Markets	Of limited importance.	Developed at the supralocal level.	Fully developed and of great importance.
Mode of Succession to Office	Predominantly hereditary.	Hereditary and by appointment.	Mainly by appointment.
Ownership of Land	Private ownership rare. Mainly communal ownership of land and livestock.	Private ownership of land limited, but increasing ownership by the state.	Private ownership of land important for both aristocracy and common people.
Judicial System	No codification of laws and punishments. No specialized formal judges.	Incipient codification of laws and punishments. Formal judges and general (nonspecialized) functionaries who decide cases.	Codification of laws and punishments complete. Administration of justice in the hands of formal judges.
Taxation	Irregular voluntary tribute and occasional labor.	Regular tribute. Major works undertaken with aid of compulsory labor.	Well-defined taxation system with complex apparatus to insure regular flow.

SOURCE: Claessen and Skalník (eds.) 1978.

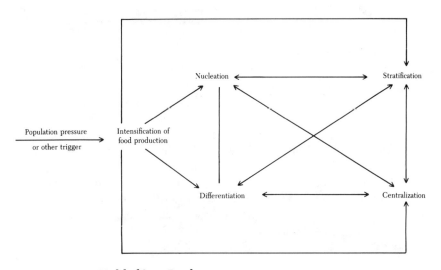

Fig. 5 *Systems Model of State Development*

SOURCE: Jolly and Plog 1979; 365, based partially on Logan and Sanders 1976.

are considered predisposing factors without which the early state is impossible.

Four factors are singled out by the authors as directly causal: (1) population growth and/or population pressure; (2) war or the threat of war; (3) conquest; and (4) the influence of previously existing states. Most early states seem to have developed out of a combination of these, interacting with each other and appearing in no particular sequence. Wittfogel's hydraulic theory is not supported, since less than half the sample was clearly dependent on extensive irrigation systems. However, both Carniero's "environmental circumscription" model and Boserup's population pressure theory would be supported, but only if assimilated into some sort of systems model in which these factors are viewed not as primary causes, but as elements interacting with many other elements. In Table 3, the characteristics of twenty-one early states are outlined.

Though no other book has gone so far in classifying the early state or in delineating its common elements, the conclusions regarding the genesis of this form of political organization seem anticlimactic. As the scope of theory broadens from the primary states to the scores of systems that can be classified as "early states," we would expect fewer generalizations to hold for the entire sample—and the influence of preexisting states is probably powerful, subtle, and immeasurable. There has been progress, of course. The search for a single dominant cause has been abandoned in favor of theories that stress the systemic interaction of many causes. One wonders, however, if systems approaches have really added that much to our understanding, since these mainly combine forces and processes that have been known for a long time. Essentially, what the systems theorists have done is raise the model of the evolution of the state to such a high level of abstraction that it is no longer easy to find exceptions to every generalization. Because of the resulting loss in specificity, one feels the need to fill in blanks in the model, to reestablish the sense that we are talking about real human beings—living, dying, warring, struggling to make it against the odds. The generalizations must be taken back to the archeological digs, to the sad pottery shards and broken amulets and old walls of lost civilizations; back to the nascent states of Africa and India where kings and peasants contended in an eternal game of conflict and accord. Theory must hold a middle position in anthropology, for ultimately everything begins and ends in the field.

SUGGESTED READINGS

Claessen, Henry J.M., and Peter Skalník (eds.)
The Early State (The Hague, Netherlands: Mouton, 1978)
This massive work (nearly 700 pages) begins with four chapters on the theory of state origins, then offers twenty chapters on individual states, and closes with four chapters synthesizing these specific studies and making cross-cultural comparisons. As a treatise on secondary state formation the book is definitive. However, it deliberately avoids the distinction between primary and secondary states and, therefore, cannot deal with some of the most basic theories of state formation.

Cohen, Ronald, and Elman R. Service (eds.)
Origins of the State: The Anthropology of Political Evolution (Philadelphia: Institute for the Study of Human Issues, 1978)
The introduction and first chapters provide brief overviews of the major theories of state formation. Two other articles strike me as especially valuable: Henry Wright's "Toward an Explanation of the Origin of the State," which puts many of the major theories in easy-to-understand flow-chart form; and Robert Carniero's application of the "principal of competitive exclusion" (from evolutionary biology) to state formation.

Harris, Marvin
Cannibals and Kings: The Origins of Cultures (New York: Vintage, 1977)
Harris covers so much territory, from cannibalism among the Aztecs to the sacred cow in India, that it is easy to forget that, as a whole, this book is a theory of state formation. Harris has been accused of sometimes stretching facts to fit his materialist theory, but even when controversial he is always entertaining.

Pfeiffer, John E.
The Emergence of Society: A Prehistory of the Establishment (New York: McGraw Hill, 1977)
This panoramic overview of cultural evolution never attained the best-seller status of the author's earlier *The Emergence of Man*, though Pfeiffer's knack for presenting hard scholarship in a popular manner is quite evident. Among other topics, the book covers the rise of domestication, state development in all six primary areas, and the diffusion of civilization.

Struever, Stuart (ed.)
Prehistoric Agriculture (Garden City, N.Y.: The Natural History Press, 1971)
The domestication of plants and animals is a crucial precursor to the evolution

of primary states. The thirty-three chapters of this anthology, written by many noted archeologists, balance both theory and fieldwork. Included is Kent Flannery's now-classic application of general systems theory to cultural evolution in Tehuacán Valley, Mexico.

An early-twentieth-century king of Cambodia draws
much of his political legitimacy from religion (Library
of Congress).

CHAPTER *4*

Religion in Politics

It may not be true, as Georges Balandier (1970:38) has contended, that the sacred is *always* present in politics; but it is seldom far away. Viewers of the classic propaganda film *Triumph of the Will*, made at the 1934 Nazi Party Conference in Nuremberg, might justifiably wonder whether they are watching a political rally or a religious ceremony. An implicit sacredness underlies the Declaration of Independence and the Constitution of the United States, and offers a divine legitimacy to political succession. In modern-day Iran and Ireland, political conflict may be indistinguishable from religious conflict. However, in preindustrial societies the boundaries of the various subsystems—political, kinship, economic, religious, etc.—are far less clearly demarcated than in more complex and specialized societies. An African candidate for headmanship who calls on ancestor spirits for support no more considers himself resorting to the "supernatural" than would a senatorial candidate in the United States who accepts a campaign contribution from a major corporation.

The role which religion plays in politics is difficult to correlate with evolutionary complexity. We find power directly based on the supernatural at all levels. Among some Eskimos, the shaman was the most powerful of men by virtue of his access to the spirit world; among the tribal Hopi of the American southwest, political power is articulated through ceremonies, dances, and religious sodalities; modern Israel is a highly industrialized and internationally powerful nation-state ultimately based on common religion and tradition. On the other hand, it would be equally easy to provide examples of hunting-gathering peoples (the !Kung, the Tasaday of the Philippines), tribal groups (the Yanomamo), and industrial states (the Soviet Union) in which religion plays relatively little part.

The role of religion and the supernatural in politics is manifested mainly in three ways: (1) the government may be directly based on religion, as in a theocracy; (2) religion may be used to legitimize the ruling elite; and (3) religion may provide the underlying structures, beliefs, and traditions which are manipulated by aspirants to power.

Sacred Legitimacy

There is no clear-cut dividing line between a theocracy and a secular state. Since virtually all preindustrial states claim at least some degree of divine legitimacy, and since even the most religiously-oriented of administrations must solve a number of very secular problems—defense, trade, development of roads and irrigation networks—the amount of religious emphasis is a matter of degree, not kind. Even in most cases where religion plays an extemely important role, the secular and priestly bureaucracies are kept quite separate (as was true, for example, for the Inca and the Maya). While the priests may have enormous power, it is not power that would usually be expended on the mundane functioning of the government. Divine kings may, like the Pope, express their divinity only on certain specific occasions and in very specific contexts. Jacobus Janssen (1978) argues that this was true of the Egyptian pharoahs, who "guaranteed and maintained the cosmic order" while at the same time being subject to that order (*Ma'at*); their persons were taboo, but they were incapable of working miracles; they were omnipotent but subject to the gods and forced to rule through purely mundane means. People in states that are not as highly segmented as our own seem to have little problem dealing with the simultaneity of the human and the divine, the sacred and the secular.

Lucy Mair notes two requisites for kingship in Africa: the support of a loyal following, and some claim on the part of the would-be king to a special relationship with supernatural beings. In other words, a king requires both secular support and sacred legitimacy. The first will derive from the individual king's personality and abilities and from his rightful claim, within traditional rules, to the throne; he must attain legitimacy through linking himself by myth to a supernatural ancestor responsible for the origin of the group or for some crucial event in the mythological history (Mair, 1962).

The Shilluk of the Sudan believe in a semi-divine cultural hero who, through an Exodus-like epic adventure, established them as a unique people, set up the first villages, and founded the basic divisions of their society. This deathless hero, Ny'ikang, simply disappeared, and his spirit enters into each succeeding king. The Shilluk were the only contemporary group chosen by James George Frazer, in his classic *The Golden Bough* (1890), to support his theory that the king represented the fertility of the land and cattle. According to Frazer, the king had to be killed in a ritual manner before he became old, in order that the mystic potency would always remain with a virile leader. While it is true that many such kings died young, in battle or through assassination, the belief that the king was ritually killed is itself part of Shilluk mythology! There are many authenticated accounts of the kingly successor being chosen by a council of chiefs. Yet Frazer, while overemphasizing the symbolic value of fertility, did hit on an important element of African kingship—the symbolic identification of the king's person with the welfare of the whole society (Mair 1962).

Religious ritual also has important political functions. The periodic reenactment of legitimizing myths unites the entire community in a sacred bond that transcends private interests and day-to-day conflicts, while re-infusing the society with the mystical power of the world of the ancestors. In some uncentralized societies, religious ceremony was the major source of tribal integration. For many of the Plains Indians, for example, it was only for two weeks during the summer Sun Dance that the entire tribe came together as a unit. It was at this time that the council of chiefs would meet and make group decisions, and when Medicine Bundles, which brought both mystical and secular power to their owners, exchanged hands.

Manipulation of Religious Symbols

The supernatural is much more than a simple set of passive beliefs that form an unchanging backdrop for political action. Such beliefs are subject to the manipulation both of individuals who compete for power, and of those who are called to support (or withold support from) the competitors. This is clearly exemplified in the political system of the Lugbara of Uganda. This group, which has a classic segmentary lineage system, lacked any formal government whatsoever prior to the colonial period. The smallest effective unit of society was the local patrilineal kinship group, consisting of a cluster of families, and in lieu of kings or chiefs, authority was vested in an age-set system. As members of the age-grades of "youth" and "big youth" grew older, they came in conflict with their elders over land and authority. Since violence was not permitted among kinsmen, generational conflicts had to be worked out by mystical means. If one of the parties in the conflict were to fall sick and the oracles showed that his opponent had conjured the ancestors to wreak sickness, the conjurer would gain power by having his authority affirmed. On the other hand, if it were believed that the dead had been invoked merely to gain or maintain status, rather than to benefit the lineage, the invoker could be accused of being a witch, and therefore lose status. These two interpretations are only narrowly different, but can have the effect of either legitimizing or destroying a person's authority. Thus, there is room here for manipulation of the belief system not only by the individuals involved, but by the public and the guardian of the oracle making the decision as well. Conflicts between local groups are not susceptible to this sort of resolution, since ghost-invocation and witchcraft are thought to be ineffective beyond the minimal lineage. Duelling, feuding, and outright warfare were common means of conflict resolution; but accusations of sorcery were often employed between close neighbors who wished to avoid open violence. In any case, all political authority was primarily supernatural, since it was controlled by the dead ancestors, and since the power of sanctions derived from the same source (Middleton 1960, 1966).

The Adaptive Value of "Deviant" Religion

So far, we have dealt with religion in its most common role, as a strongly conservative force in society. However, religion can also be an important progressive element. The Aymara Indians living in the community of Soqa, in the Lake Titicaca region of Peru, were first missionized by Seventh-Day Adventists around 1915. At that time, most Aymara followed their traditional earth-mother religion. (They had adopted from Catholicism a few saints and the Virgin Mary, who had simply been added to the indigenous pantheon, and a fiesta system that consisted largely of dancing and getting falling-down drunk for a few days every year.) The Aymara were economically self-sufficient, monolingual, and cut off from any but the most cursory market relations with the exploitive *mestizo* class. The Seventh-Day Adventists, after many years of utter failure, established a mission in a small village and began to offer their religion as a package deal: health, education, Jesus—in that order. Contrary to the usual theory, it was not the cultural deviants, but the more intellectually-oriented, often community leaders, who were willing to try the package (which in practice meant abstinence from alcohol, some degree of modern medical aid, and sufficient education to learn to read the Spanish-language Bible and hymnal). To the north of the lake, where literacy threatened the hacienda system, there were many murders and burnings of Adventist churches, but the worst that happened to the free-holding Adventists near the lake was that they were once beaten and dragged off to jail. Generally, persecution consisted of Adventist-baiting, such as capturing them at fiesta time and forceably pouring liquor down their throats until they were drunk. Though persecution was relatively mild, it was constant; the small group was ostracized, their formal leaders lost all authority, and so the situation remained for almost four decades.

The political system at that time was based on the *ayllu*, discussed earlier (Chapter 2). Over the centuries, many *ayllus* had become so loosely structured that they were held together largely by means of numerous and proliferating fiestas throughout the year. These fiestas provided both leadership, through sponsors, and an excuse to come together as a unified social and political group. However, in the early 1950s, as population began to overgrow the carrying capacity of the land for subsistence farming, the fiesta system with its enormous outlays by sponsors became too expensive to be maintained. In 1955, with a federal government engineer as guide, young progressives replaced the *ayllu* system with a community-based political structure, complete with mayor, vice-mayor, and lieutenants. This radical transformation, considered and decided by democratic means, accomplished two important things for the handful of Seventh-Day Adventists on the island. First, since the mayor was directly responsible to the provincial governor and the vice-mayor was directly responsible to the commandant of the regional army post, formal lines of communication were established between Soqa and the *mestizo* world. Second, the end of the *ayllu*, which had been held together by the Catholic fiesta system, meant the secularization of local government for the first time in centuries. The Seventh-Day Adventists, who had been persecuted and ostracized for three generations, had also been educating themselves all that time. They were the only ones in the community who could read and write Spanish. And since they had fought for their right to practice their religion in the halls of government as far away as Lima, they were experienced in dealing with the national bureaucracy. Naturally, the Adventists quickly stepped into both formal and informal positions of power in the new Soqa government. Their unique abilities allowed them to act as culture brokers during this time of transition from a subsistence-agriculture economy to a money economy. At this writing, the long-despised Adventists continue to hold a monopoly of political power in numerous communities throughout the Peruvian *altiplano*. Since Adventist schools tend to be vastly superior to public schools, the power derived from education will probably be retained for many years—perhaps generations—to come (Lewellen 1978, 1979).

The Aymara study shows how a "deviant" religion, such as Protestantism in a traditional Catholic society, can provide the pool of variability necessary for adaptive change. In future chapters, we will examine the progressive role of religion in providing a new center for ethnic groups threatened with dissolution by processes of modernization.

SUGGESTED READINGS

Lanternari, Vittorio
The Religions of the Oppressed (New York: New American Library, 1963)
Though written by a historian, this book deserves mention here because of its basically anthropological and political point of view. The author interprets prophetic and messianic movements, such as the Peyote Cult of the American Southwest and the many cargo cults of Melanesia, as "cries for freedom" of oppressed peoples.

Middleton, John
Lugbara Religion (London: Oxford University Press, 1960)
The Lugbara of Uganda lack any formal political institutions, so power and authority are manipulated through oracles, divination, witchcraft, and sorcery. Middleton's analysis is minute and masterful.

Packard, Randall M.
Chiefship and Cosmology: An Historical Study of Political Competition (Bloomington: Indiana University Press, 1981)
In contrast to Middleton's synchronic analysis, this study of the interrelation between politics and religion among the Bashu of Zaire is very much of the process school. The author not only shows the ritual functions of chiefship today, but also traces the historical adaptations that have taken place over the last century and a half.

Swanson, Guy E.
The Birth of the Gods (Ann Arbor: University of Michigan Press, 1960)
This is the first major cross-cultural statistical study of religion to take an evolutionary approach. Some of Swanson's conclusions have been challenged by more recent research, but this book remains valuable for relating religious types to levels of political integration.

A cannon squad in revolutionary Mexico. True revolutions have been rare in Latin America (Library of Congress).

CHAPTER 5

Political Succession

Power must be counted among the scarcest of resources, and the most desirable. While it may not be useful to posit a Political Man who always maximizes his power over others, in the same way that economists have created an abstract Economic Man who always maximizes profit, there always seem to be sufficient power-oriented individuals who are willing to fight for that tiny room at the top, a room that is almost always occupied by just one individual at a time. Though government-by-committee is often tried, it is extremely unstable, as the Founding Fathers must have known when they wrote a strong presidency into the constitution (a presidency which, it might be noted, grows stronger as society becomes increasingly complex).

Just as there is usually a single leader, there tend to be many in the second position. If there were only one person next in line to leadership, that person would be very dangerous. Far better to keep a group of princes with relatively equal power in a constant state of rivalry. There are other advantages to not being overly specific in regard to who will succeed the leader. If the rules are too rigid—if the first-born son inherits leadership, for example—the state might end up in the hands of a child, a weakling, a madman, or an idiot (European history provides examples of all of these). A power struggle is an excellent way for various competitors to show their stuff in manipulating public opinion, gaining support of various factions, killing rivals, making war, and otherwise proving themselves capable of meeting the requirements of the job. As Max Gluckman (1960, 1969) pointed out, a society can actually be strengthened by rebellion and conflict because they resolve tensions and bring the strongest to prominence. For this reason, automatic succession—as in the United States—is rare in history.

Unless the rules of succession are carefully spelled out, however, that period between the death of the old king and the crowning of the new is extremely precarious for the group as a whole. A state recently formed out of a number of chiefdoms might revert to smaller units. Moreover, if two competitors can garner relatively equal support, there will almost certainly be civil war. Thus, too much rigidity in political succession will threaten the polity because of weakness at the top; too much flexibility may rend it in pieces. This is the fundamental problem of political succession. Through history it has been answered in five different ways (or in combinations of these five): diffused leadership, hereditary succession, republican government, periodic military intervention, and government-by-committee.

Diffused Leadership

In band and tribal societies, the problem of succession to leadership positions is solved very easily: there is no succession—at least not in the sense of power being passed from one person to another. With the death of a leader, so dies his power; and any contender must build a power base from scratch. As we have seen, in hunting-gathering bands leadership may be situational, and will in any case be minimal. What power exists beyond the family is confined more to arbitrating decisions than to making them, and leadership is based on personal characteristics or abilities which cannot be transferred. This is also true in horticultural or pastoral tribes, though here power may be more actively sought and there may be well defined rules of the game.

Among the Siuai of the Solomon Islands in the South Pacific, an aspiring "big man" has to collect as many wives as possible in order to form alliances with other families and to provide an ongoing visible symbol of status. In addition, pigs must be accumulated, and the taro to feed them must be grown, so that they can be used in competitive feasts designed to humiliate rivals while enlisting followers. If a few hundred men can be recruited—through force of personality, generosity and perhaps success in war—to build a large "clubhouse," status will be fairly assured, though it must then be constantly maintained against usurpers. The process tends to snowball: the more power one has, the more followers are attracted, and the more pigs can be rounded up for a feast which will in turn attract more followers and more glory. Some of these "big men" have garnered considerable power, complete with semi-redistributional economies and the ability to make war. However, loyalties remain focused solely on the individual. His lineage establishes no permanent superiority through his actions, so with his death the whole structure collapses, and loyalties are shifted to another, or several other, power-seekers (Burling 1974:14–17).

This is another demonstration of one of the defining differences between uncentralized and centralized systems; in the former, a leader— no matter how powerful—can neither pass on power nor build upon that of a predecessor.

Hereditary Succession

Political succession in chiefdoms and early states is almost invariably hereditary, which simply reflects the emphasis on kinship, especially unilineal kinship, at this mid-level in political complexity. In fact, unilineal kinship systems can be seen as the foundation upon which centralized societies are originally constructed. As the state increases in complexity and requires that its administrators possess specialized knowledge and skills, kinship will be gradually overridden as the dominant force in politics.

Table 4 shows some of the available alternatives in political succession, with a focus on hereditary systems in chiefdoms and early states. Within hereditary systems, both extremes are usually avoided: no single person (e.g., eldest son) is designated as successor, but neither are all males within the lineage eligible. Succession is circumscribed by rules which restrict the number of contenders, while providing a sufficiently large "pool of variability" (to borrow a concept from evolutionary biology) from which "the fittest" might emerge.

Martin Southwold's (1966) historical analysis of political succession among the Buganda of Uganda prior to the establishment of the British Protectorate in 1894, reveals the complexity of the succession process, even in a hereditary system. The Buganda bureaucracy consisted of a powerful, but not divine, king; a "prime-minister" who was a commoner; an aide to the king, who was also a commoner but who took the leading role in choosing the king's successor; and a series of chiefs and subchiefs who administered the various territorial divisions of the country. There were about fifty patrilineal clans, including the "royal clan" of the king,

Table 4 Succession Alternatives in Chiefdoms and Early States

	Major Strength	Major Weakness	Comments
One Ruler	More efficient; stronger in competitive situations	Disunity and competition during period of succession	In centralized political systems there seems to be a tendency for one person to dominate even in systems designed around collective leadership; thus, true collective leadership is rare
vs			
Collective Leadership	May be more responsible to group demands; no power vacuum during periods of succession	Unstable because of competition within group; cannot make decisions quickly in periods of emergency	
Heredity	In early states with unilineal kinship, descent forms a natural power base that is economically interdependent; this prevents free-for-all during succession	Other kin groups may not support system because of lack of access to power	Hereditary succession is virtually universal among early states; a lack of such legitimate succession is a major difference between "big man" tribal systems and centralized systems
vs			
Nonhereditary Succession	Allows wider range of leadership potential, gives all equal access to power	Society liable to be dismembered during period of succession because of many competitors	
General Inheritance of Power	Provides a wider range of leadership options	Creates competition among all kinsmen of noble lineage, thus disruptive to the kinship system, which is basis of royal power	General inheritance would be so unstable as to be virtually nonexistent; all hereditary polities restrict succession to certain kin only
vs			
Restricted Inheritance	Reduces competition for office	May prevent natural leaders from assuming office	
Patrilineal Succession (Restricted)	Men hold power; succession is to sons; more direct	In a matrilineal system, patrilineal descent will cross kin-group lines and confuse loyalties	Patrilineal succession is found in matrilineal societies because it is more direct; nowhere would we expect to find matrilineal succession in a patrilineal society
vs			
Matrilineal Succession	In a matrilineal society, matrilineal succession would maintain power within a single lineage	Succession would pass from leader to nephews, of which there might be a great many; indirect	

Fraternal Succession	Less likely a child will come to power if king dies young; less competition for power since younger brothers are still in line to succeed	Who succeeds to power on the death of the last brother? Creates competition among sons of all brothers	These categories are not mutually exclusive; filial succession may be temporarily replaced by fraternal succession if there is no heir or if a child inherits the throne
vs	Competition limited to a few, leadership typically younger than in fraternal succession	Possibility of a child inheriting the throne or of no heirs at all	
Filial Succession			
Designated Succession	Eliminates competition and threat of disunity during period of succession	Weak and incompetent persons can automatically attain kingship	Rules of priority usually limit succession struggles, but entirely determinant succession is rare since such a principle would ignore personal qualities of leadership
vs	Permits the "best man" (i.e., the strongest) to attain power	If too many competitors, chaos threatens; competition needs to be tempered by rules of eligibility	
Free Competition for Leadership			

SOURCE: Burling 1974:46–52.

though the latter had no totemic animal and was less formally inclusive than the others. Clan membership, though normal, was not automatic; one had to be "accepted" by the clan chief in order to belong. This fact gave clanship a selective character and made clans important political factions.

Southwold distinguishes five categories of "rules," customs, and principles by which a successor to the king was chosen: (1) prescriptive rules; (2) preferential rules; (3) personality factors; (4) political factors; and (5) the electoral institutions. *Prescriptive rules* are those held consciously by the people themselves. The primary such rule was that, although all descendants of the king were counted among the "royals," only the "Princes of the Drum" (the sons and grandsons of the king) were eligible for the highest office. In addition, the first-born son of the king was ineligible, and grandsons could only be selected if all eligible sons were dead. It was the responsibility of the "prime minister" to care for the sons of the chief, and he would make recommendations, based on the *personality factors* of the contenders, to the aide who was most responsible for selecting a successor. One son who liked to torture mice and small birds was rejected, for example, on the entirely reasonable assumption that he might prove cruel to the people. The ideal personality type was one who was restrained and humble. Commoners held the ultimate power to choose the king, and they would be careful to make sure his power was not too centralized. Many *political factors*, then, were involved in the selection. Since "Princes of the Drum" were ineligible for any office but king, and therefore in direct and intense competition within their own lineage, they would usually turn to their mothers' lineages for support, specifically to their mothers' brothers who might hold power as chiefs or subchiefs. This meant that the power and influence of each mother's clan was a primary consideration in the king's selection. Also of prime importance were the *electoral institutions* themselves; though the king's aide had the greatest voice, many other commoner and royal chiefs were involved in the process, and their opinions and strengths had to be considered.

All this is somewhat ideal, since it is based on the assumption that it really was the sons that inherited the kingship, that the prescriptive rules were actually followed. However, by analyzing the actual list of kings, Southwold found that often, especially during a certain extended period, succession was fraternal rather than filial, and the mode of succession was rebellion rather than election. In other words, outside the prescriptive rules was a set of *preferential rules*, one of which stipulated that in periods when maturity and strength were important, brothers were preferred over inexperienced sons.

The Latin American Model

Though the republican (or representative democracy) form of succession has been analyzed by anthropologists, as has the collective leadership of the Soviet Union and other communist countries, such modern forms of nation-state rule continue to be more within the domain of political science than political anthropology. We will look at some of the anthropological perspectives on industrial-state governments in a later chapter. However, we include here a discussion of Latin American politics; even at the national level it has been of perennial interest to anthropologists who could hardly ignore the effects of national policies on native peoples.

The peaceful succession which Western democratic nations consider "normal," may in fact be the norm neither within the vast span of history nor in most modern-day developing countries. It is common knowledge that the turmoil of recent African history derives from the fact that these nations are "new," having gained their independence from the colonial powers only after World War II, and that things will settle down as these nations mature. But a glance at Latin America reveals that such expectations may be mere wishful thinking. Latin America has had more than a century and a half of independence, yet violence continues to be virtually the legitimate means for the transfer of power, and governments may change types—from *caudillo* to oligarchy rule, from military dictatorship to representative democracy, from one-man rule to junta—as often as they change leaders.

The reasons for this political volatility are legion, but certainly history accounts for a great deal of it. The conquest of North America was accomplished through settlement by vast numbers of immigrants who claimed the land and worked it themselves (or brought in slaves from Africa to work it), and virtual genocide against the native population. In Latin America, with the exception of coastal Brazil and the southernmost countries, the land was viewed as a supplier of raw materials to Spain; thus the Indians were left in place to work vast tracts of land given to *conquistadores* for their service to Church and Crown. As a result, arable land—and thus wealth—was concentrated in the hands of very few families right from the beginning. Much of the population remained traditionally "Indian," living in closed peasant communities with their own language and folk culture. Over time, intermarriage between Indians and the Spanish conquerors produced an intermediate class of *mestizos*. In colonial times, all higher government offices were held by Spanish administrators, and *creoles* (American-born "Europeans") had to make do with local-level councils drawn from the richer families. With the coming of independence, the only experience that the *creoles* had with government was within these weak and ineffective councils, which often were quickly dominated by strong "men on horseback" who possessed sufficient charisma to develop militant personal followings. Throughout the nineteenth century and much of the twentieth, these *caudillos* have dominated Latin American politics at all levels.

National leaders of the *caudillo* stripe, such as Juan Peron of Argentina, play at politics in a strongly personalistic way and often draw their power from appeals to the workers, or to some working-class segment of society. A "dictator" is a slightly different phenomenon; men like Somoza in Nicaragua, Trujillo in the Dominican Republic, and Batista in Cuba were skilled in manipulating the richer elements of the society, in forming personal armies, and especially in using the United States' paranoia of Communism to centralize enormous wealth and power. They made only nominal concessions to the masses.

Few dictators have held absolute power, at least in the early years of their rule. A basic job requirement is the ability to balance many forces within the country while simultaneously juggling rival claims and rival interests. Historically, the two key forces have been the oligarchy and the army, either of which might assume the reins of government. Oligarchies originally consisted of the landed elite. In many countries, such as Peru and Uruguay, the big money has been shifted from land to industry with the result that it is no longer possible to speak of a few families who control most of the arable land. Today, elites are formed out of agrarian-industrial complexes with close ties to multinational corporations based in the United States, Europe, and Japan. There is a symbiotic relationship between the army and the elite in these countries; most of the officers (often either trained in the United States, or by advisors from the United States) come from the elite. At the same time, the army has a degree of autonomy which it jealously guards. Armies have not always acted predictably—they have sometimes been willing to step aside to civilian rule, to allow total chaos to develop (as in Argentina) before assuming dictatorial power, and even to impose extensive popular reforms (as in the Velasco government in Peru). In contrast to the developed western countries, however, the army is autonomous of any government it does not itself run.

All Latin American governments have constitutions. Some have closets full of constitutions, abrogated and rewritten as often as governments change. Since these countries lack any real commitment to constitutional succession, have long repudiated the idea of hereditary leadership, and possess massive illiterate and semi-literate populations which often identify more with an ethnic group than the state, it is little wonder that the more peaceful means of political succession have so seldom found favor in Latin American countries. In the absence of any direct means of popular input, the primary goal of government has been to protect the wealth of the elite and the power of the military. Of course, adjustments are made as deemed necessary to suppress popular discontent; these can range from agrarian reform and minimum wage laws to brutal represssion.

Eric Wolf and Edward Hansen (1972) have developed a typology of Latin American succession. "*Machetismo*" refers to the process, long the norm at the local rural level, by which one *caudillo* is able to garner enough bald power to impose his absolute will through a following of armed men (in the nineteenth century, often cane workers armed with machetes). When raised to the national level, this type of succession may involve scores of regional strong men, each with his own private army, fighting to attain the status of *jefe maximo:* one such conflict in Colombia between 1899 and 1903 cost 100,000 lives. "*Cuartelezco*" refers to a barracks rebellion (*cuartel* = barracks). The classic pattern is for one group of military officers to coordinate simultaneous attacks on communication centers, military supplies, and the seat of government, immediately followed by the announcement of a new junta and of reforms. If carried out smoothly, at a time when the standing government is sufficiently unpopular and is alienated from the military, such a change of power may be relatively bloodless. A "*golpe de estado*" (the Spanish phrasing of "*coup d'etat*") may even bypass the military completely; it strikes directly at the seat of power, through either the assassination or the detention of the president.

The obvious problem with such violent means of succession is that the new government may possess little in the way of legitimacy in the eyes of the people. One method of gaining such legitimacy is to sponsor an *election;* this will have the added advantage of providing the elected government (assuming it is allowed to come to power) with a friendly pat on the back from the United States. Most countries in Latin America have tried this form at least once, but it has not proved especially stable. However, the legitimacy of an election can be contrived to some degree through *imposición,* a process by which the ruling forces hand-pick a candidate and rig the election to make sure he wins; or by "*candidato unico,*" in which the ruler holds an election with himself as the sole candidate. A more subtle approach to extending the legitimizing dictatorial power is "*continuismo,*" by which a president's term of office will be extended through manipulation of the existing constitution, by writing a new constitution, by new legislation, or by a favorable judicial ruling.

All of the more violent forms of political succession are what Max Gluckman (1960) would have called "rebellion": the head of state changes, but the system remains intact. True revolution—actual structural change in the system itself—has occurred only in Mexico, Cuba, and Nicaragua. This is not to say that massive changes have not taken place in virtually all Latin American countries; but in the majority (and this may be true, to a great degree, of Mexico also) these changes are more in the line of adaptive adjustments that have permitted the old economic structures to remain intact through making some, often minimal, concessions to popular unrest.

SUGGESTED READINGS

Burling, Robbins
The Passage of Power: Studies in Political Succession (New York: Academic Press, 1974)
The introduction and conclusions provide a theoretical framework for the specific studies of political succession that make up the body of the book. Included are the Marathas of India, Manchu China, Latin America, and contemporary Eastern Europe and the Soviet Union. The depth and range of Burling's research is impressive.

Goody, Jack (ed.)
Succession to High Office (Cambridge: Cambridge University Press, 1966)
In contrast to Burling, who uses only state-level examples, Goody focuses on more conventionally anthropological subjects, namely, chiefdoms and incipient states in Africa. The four articles are written for a professional audience, but make for worthwhile reading if one is willing to wade through some complex kinship diagrams. In contrast, Goody's introduction is a straightforward typology and model of succession in preindustrial African systems.

Early structural-functionalists often ignored the colonial context of their studies. Here a native king is flogged by British colonial soldiers (Library of Congress).

CHAPTER 6

Structure and Process

"Structure may go to the wall," wrote F.G. Bailey in 1968, "but people survive." This could have been the rally cry for an entire generation of political anthropologists who, during the 1950s and 1960s, guided the transition from the study of norms, values, and atemporal social structures to an emphasis on competition, conflict, history, and change. The paradigm so self-consciously and often vehemently repudiated was the "structural-functionalism" of A.R. Radcliffe-Brown, which had dominated British anthropology for more than twenty years. Since the "new" political anthropology is to a great degree a reaction to this theoretical orientation, it is worthwhile to take a critical look at it.

Structural-Functionalism

If one were to reduce the structural-functionalist position to only four words or phrases, they might be *synchronic, teleological, Africa,* and *closed system.* The term "synchronic" is defined by Webster as "concerned with the complex of events existing in a limited time period and ignoring historical antecedent." This would be the definition favored by the critics of structural-funcionalism, who constantly complained that societies were ripped out of their historical context and treated as though

85

they were static over long periods. Yet in reality the early political anthropologists did not so much portray their societies as excessively stable or unchanging (though this might be implied from their method of analysis), but rather as *outside of time*, in the same way that a still photograph captures an instant without denying temporal processes. And just as a still photograph may suggest a great deal of movement, as well as a past and a future, the structural-functionalists allowed for all sorts of tensions and conflicts within their frame of reference.

In a sense, then, we might think of these researchers as comparable to intelligence personnel who analyze aerial photographs. They tried to look at society "from above," as a whole, and to map the interconnections between the various subsystems of the society—kinship, marriage, religion, politics. The society itself was considered not only outside of time, but also isolated in space. Though a tribe or chiefdom might be contained within a nation state, it was viewed as a thing unto itself, relatively independent of its wider social environment; that is, as a *closed system* with its own culture, its own values, its own mechanisms of adjustment.

The question immediately arises: adjustment to what purpose? The structural-functionalists had a ready answer: adjustment to the equilibrium of the whole. Far from being static, institutions within the society were constantly changing shape—as smaller groups formed and reformed, as alliances were made, as feuds and wars were fought—but all of these were interpreted as contributions to the integrity of the whole. Thus, any particular institution was analyzed in regard to the way that it functioned to aid the survival of the larger system. In this sense, structural-functionalist causality was the reverse of Aristotelian causality; effects were not pushed from behind, so to speak, but pulled from in front. One would not explain a religious ritual in terms of its historical development but rather in terms of its purpose or function, which was ultimately the maintenance of societal equilibrium. In short, institutions and activities were analyzed teleologically (i.e., in terms of a goal toward which they were directed). It was recognized, of course, that the people themselves would offer completely different reasons for their behavior; but these *manifest functions*, while certainly important and often recorded in great detail, were not analytically significant. The anthropologist was much more interested in the *latent functions*, of which individuals were unaware, and these could only be determined by looking at the whole system (just as, for example, the liver can only be understood in relation to the survival of the body).

One reason that this paradigm could be sustained for so long was that virtually all fieldwork was done in the part of Africa that was under British colonial rule, where cultures remained separated by language barriers, distinctive cultural patterns, and the paternalistic prejudices of the ruling class of British administrators. Also, there was a tendency to seek out for fieldwork the more "typical" villages—those which were most traditional—and to use these to represent the entire language group. This naturally had the effect of minimizing culture contact.

All of these elements are either implicit or explicit in E.E. Evans-Pritchard's classic *The Nuer* (1940). The basic goal of the book, including a chapter on the political system, was to show how a society of 200,000 people could maintain equilibrium despite almost constant feuding and an utter lack of any kind of centralized government. Radcliffe-Brown's explanation, based on the concept of "complementary opposition" (which we discussed in Chapter 3), demonstrates how the equilibrium of the whole can be maintained, not just in spite of conflicting parts, but actually as a result of them.

It is no accident that the demise of structural-functionalism coincided almost exactly with the demise of British colonialism after World War II. The synchronic approach required a fairly clear still photograph, and the image tended to blur when the action got too chaotic or when too many different groups crowded into the frame. The repudiation of structural-functionalism began blandly enough, but quickly turned to revolution, with all of the vehemence radical change seems to require. Most of the criticisms now seem rather obvious: societies are not in equilibrium; teleological arguments are not scientific; no society is isolated from its social surroundings; societies are not homogenous; colonial Africa is not the world. Structural-functionalism, and British anthropology as a whole, were accused of having been servants of colonialism. Perhaps the most telling criticism was simply that the theory had become routinized and was threatening to degenerate into a mindless game in which one could point out, with a semblance of great profundity, that a religious ritual brought lots of people together and thus maintained social equilibrium.

All these objections are justified. "Process" does indeed stand triumphant over the corpse of "equilibrium." But it is possible to look back from the vantage of victory and discern in the defeated enemy certain admirable qualities that were not visible during the smoke of battle. In retrospect, a book like *The Nuer* seems an enduringly brilliant and perceptive piece of analysis. The idealized portraits painted by the structural-functionalists of entire societies are very close to pictures of what is now being called "political culture"—that set of values and interactions common to a traditional society. In this respect, structural-functionalism seems close to the symbolist school of political anthropology, which views culture, including politics, as involving powerful sets of unconscious symbols. These symbols form a setting in which political action takes place;

what has been added is the emphasis on the ways in which symbols are used and manipulated by individual actors. Even in the midst of the repudiation of structural-functionalism, one of the pioneers of the new process school, F.G. Bailey (1960:240), felt it necessary to caution his colleagues, "I cannot emphasize too strongly that without the fixed points which are provided by a static structural analysis, we have no means of describing the change that is taking place."

The idea of latent functions has been taken over, virtually intact, by ecological anthropologists, who view societies as unconsciously adjusting to maintain ecological balance. Teleology, once considered one of the nastiest words in science, has been incorporated into both biology and physics and has now moved, via general systems theory, into the social sciences, where goal-direction may be legitimately viewed as a prime force for both individuals *and* groups. Also from general systems theory comes the concept of "boundaries," the defining qualities of a social system, which block or filter input from outside the system. Within these boundaries, constant adjustments are taking place to maintain the system, but the boundaries themselves may be stable for long periods of time. It should be obvious that, *for a relatively closed system*, the picture one gets from applying the concepts of general systems theory are not especially different from that of the structural-functionalists. While the superiority of a process approach cannot be denied—if only because its scope is so much wider and its analytical tools so much more diverse—there is indeed in society something that is continuous, something that forms the backdrop for change. This is what the structural-functionalists were able to describe with such perception.

The Process Approach

It is easy, in retrospect, to impose too much coherence on the reaction against structural-functionalism, to suppose that these writers had some philosophical view in common and were all moving in the same direction. Actually, their explorations could hardly have been more varied. Turner's *Schism and Continuity in an African Society* (1957) and Edmund Leach's *Political Systems of Highland Burma* (1954) represent opposite poles, one focusing on a few individuals in one small village, the other on ethnic populations interacting within a modern nation state. Perhaps the only thing these two seminal works have in common is that both seem to cling to the old paradigm with one hand while feeling their way toward a new paradigm with the other. In fact, the field situation itself—whether uniform in population or of great ethnic diversity, whether tribal or state, in conflict or at peace—was much more significant in determining the line of analysis than any common theoretical point of view.

It is a curious fact of political anthropology that its major "position papers" are often contained in relatively brief introductions to anthologies. In 1940, the Introduction to *African Political Systems* provided the stimulus and theoretical basis for the first generation of political anthropologists. In 1966, three writers who were in the forefront of the reaction against structural-functionalism—Marc Swartz, Victor Turner, and Arthur Tuden—codified the foundation concepts for a generation of "process theorists" in their Introduction to *Political Anthropology*.

For these authors, the study of politics "is the study of the *processes* involved in determining and implementing public goals and in the differential achievement and use of power by the members of the group concerned with these goals" (Swartz, Turner, & Tuden 1966:7). There are several key words in this tight definition. The emphasis on process is obvious, but the political anthropologist is only concerned with *public* processes, involving an entire group. This provides an escape from overgeneralized views of politics or power which seem to include almost any relation of power, even at the level of the family; but still it leaves enough flexibility to include neighborhood or nation. The concept of *goals* has taken a marked shift from the orientation of the synchronic analysts, who were interested mainly in the "latent" functions that led to the goal of "equilibrium" or survival. The new group of writers are much more interested in the consciously held goals of the group, whether they be lower taxes, better roads, or leadership in war. The ability to make and enforce such decisions constitutes power. Political anthropology thus consists mainly in the study of the *competition for power*, and the way that *group goals are implemented* by those possessing power.

Three broad trends are now discernible. First, "process" became the key word of political anthropology as societies were studied in their historical, or at least temporal, context; thus, the emphasis was shifted from equilibrium to change. Second, a significant group of researchers narrowed their focus to a sharp concentration on the activities of individuals vying for power within very limited political settings. Third, another group of researchers broadened the perspective to include the national system, with a strong emphasis on the adaptive changes traditional cultures must make as they are incorporated politically into the modern industrial state; sometimes the state government itself is the subject of analysis. The three theoretical perspectives are summarized in Table 5. Though these three trends are intertwined, each is distinctive

Table 5 Three Theoretical Perspectives in Political Anthropology

	Structural-Functionalism	The Process Approach	
		Process Theory	Action Theory
Goals	To show how particular institutions serve to maintain the equilibrium of the whole society	To define the processes involved in political competitions and in implementing public goals	To describe individual strategies for gaining and maintaining power
Unit of Analysis	A society, tribe, social group, etc., usually treated as an ideal whole; this group was considered for analytical purposes as a closed system insofar as little regard was paid to the wider environment	The "political field," a flexible and relative concept referring to any area in which political interaction takes place; may involve a part of society or extend beyond social or ethnic boundaries	The "political arena," an area in which individual actors or small groups vie for political power. Political arenas may be, or be comprised all or in part of, factions, patron-client relations, parties, elites, and other informal parapolitical groups
Analytic Approach to Time	Synchronic: society is viewed as though outside of time, in ideal present	Diachronic, or "in time": analysis may focus on actual history or on ideal processes of change through time	Diachronic, but often focused on the actions of individuals within the duration of the anthropologist's fieldwork
Attitude toward Change	In some writings, there was simply no interest expressed in change; society was treated in a purely structural fashion; in other writings, change (in the sense of adaptive adjustments of the parts) was emphasized, but the whole was seen to be in equilibrium	Conflict, tension, and change are viewed as the normal condition of society	Change within a political arena is virtually constant, though there may be a relative stability of the wider system
Key Terms	Structure, function, equilibrium, integration	Process, competition, conflict, power, legitimacy, support	Strategy, manipulation, decision making, roles, goals, games, rules
Examples	African Political Systems, ed. Fortes and Evans-Pritchard; The Nuer, by Evans-Pritchard	Political Systems of Highland Burma, by Leach (transitional); Political Anthropology, ed. Swartz, Turner, and Tuden	Schism and Continuity in an African Society, by Turner; Lugbara Religion, by Middleton; "Political Anthropology: Manipulative Strategies," by Vincent, in Annual Review of Anthropology 1978

enough to deserve its own chapter. The remainder of this chapter will focus on the general elements of what has come to be known as "process theory," but is better referred to as the "process approach".

Field and Arena

The unit of study was formerly a specifiable group, even if that group was not always well defined. Anthropologists examined political structures within a village, a lineage, a clan, a tribe—even sometimes a "culture" (usually meaning a particular language group). Unfortunately, politics does not confine itself so neatly to such social units, and even if we were able to discover the locus of political behavior within a society, it may not stay put. For example, if we were to examine a medium-size American town over time, we would find that most people were both apathetic and ignorant about the day-to-day running of the government. Local elections would create factions, but these might encompass only a minority of the citizens. "Hot" issues, such as busing to attain racial balance in the schools, or a threatened police strike, might involve almost the entire community. Periodically, the people would be drawn into statewide elections and statewide political problems, and every four years most of the people would become involved in national politics along with local politicians trying to get a grip on the encumbered coattails of one or another presidential candidate.

This recognition—that political structures overlap but do not coincide with other social structures, and that they tend to wax and wane over time—led to the concept of the *political field*. The structural-functionalists seemed to conceptualize politics as a one-set stage play; there might be hints of a wider world, but the action was confined within a coherent and specifiable environment. Process theorists tend to view politics more in the sense of a passion play: there is an ongoing coherence of plot, and the same actors and groups may participate continuously, but the action shifts from area to area over time. This would be the political field, a fluid area of dynamic tension in which political decision making and competition takes place. To return to our passion-play analogy, much of the action would involve broad scope and grandeur, but periodically the drama would narrow to a sharp focus on two or a few actors. While these actors might be essential to the story line, their actions could only be understood in relation to the wider setting. In this case, out of the whole field we would have chosen to concentrate our attention on one small *arena*.

Actually, the concepts of political field and political arena remain ill-defined. Some writers use the terms interchangeably; others have very specific meanings in mind. F.G. Bailey (1969), for example, considers a political field as one in which the rival groups do *not* share agreed-on rules for regulating their conflict; he sees an arena as an area in which the same rules are accepted by the various competitors. Pragmatically, the very relativism of the two concepts is their primary virtue. A political field is nothing less, or more, than the wider area of political activity *defined by a particular researcher*, while an arena is an area within the field on which the researcher wants to concentrate at a particular moment. While these concepts are quite relative, they need not be arbitrary; different fieldworkers in the same society might choose to concentrate on different levels of political interaction, but they would probably have little trouble agreeing (to the extent that anthropologists agree on anything) on the boundaries of the various levels. With the concepts of "field" and "arena," we both allow and insist that the researcher precisely define that aspect of the social system which has been separated out as the unit of analysis.

Power

A Maori shaman cures meningitis through an infusion of an invisible force—*mana*—into the body of his patient. A Cree Indian chief plans a wedding. A United States president unleashes a bombing of unprecedented scope on a small, backward Asian country. A Lugbara sorcerer invokes ghosts to inflict sickness upon a neighbor. An Aztec priest tears the living heart from a human sacrifice.

What these disparate actions have in common is that they all exemplify the use of *power*. In the first case, the shaman's power is impersonal and supernatural. The United States' role in Vietnam was a case of the direct application of massive force by an advanced industrial society upon a peasant state. Among the egalitarian Cree Indians, planning a wedding is one of the few areas in which the "chief" is permitted to exercise authority and demonstrate his leadership. For the Lugbara, actual sorcery, as well as making accusations of sorcery and witchcraft, is a common means of manipulating public opinion to gain political support. Finally, for the Aztec, the priest became the servant of enormous power of religious tradition.

Any concept which must encompass such a range of situations can hardly be defined in too narrow a fashion. Power does not come from physical force alone. During the Iranian revolution, the Shah had direct access to the best modern weaponry that state's enormous oil riches could buy, as well as to an efficient police apparatus skilled in murder and torture; yet the real power, it emerged, belonged to the Ayatollah Khomeini, a fundamentalist Islamic holy man with neither weapons nor troops. Even in the United States, the President, who as Chief of the Armed Forces commands great world power, may lose that power simply because his right to hold office has come into question, as the Watergate incident so aptly illustrated. This is not to say that power cannot exist independent of public support; indeed, at this writing, governments whose right to rule rests to some extent on their control of death squads and torture chambers exist in Argentina, Chile, Uruguay, Guatemala, El Salvador, Bolivia, and Paraguay—to name just those countries in our own hemisphere. Any definition of power must include both that which is based on force and that which is not, that which derives from the individual and that which derives from a system or an office.

Ronald Cohen (1970:31) defines power as "an ability to influence the behavior of others and/or gain influence over the control of valued actions." This is broad enough to include the gamut of our examples, but requires that we further distinguish between "private" power (e.g., power exercised by a domineering father over his family) and "public" power, which is exercised in the political arena. It is the latter that is of interest to the political anthropologist.

Power may be independent or dependent (Adams 1973). *Independent power* is a relation of dominance based on the direct capabilities of an individual, such as special knowledge, skills, or personal "charisma." Many North American and Oceanic societies conceive of power as an objective force inherent in individuals. Everyone possesses some of this force, but real power relationships come into being when one individual is recognized to have more of the kind that is needed for group decision making. In egalitarian societies, at the band and tribal levels of political development, such personal qualities will be the primary means by which one person gains influence over the group, an influence that is usually limited to arbitrating disputes or setting an example. In more centralized societies, independent power may become objectified and formalized, attaching to a particular office, no matter who holds that office; also, it may give rise to extremes of political domination, as we see in the elaborate ritual and taboos surrounding the divine Inca, the ancient Hawaiian chiefs, or even the emperor of Japan. While these extreme examples may be foreign to American democratic values, in reality everyone is constantly assessing the "power" of those with whom they come into contact and adjusting their behavior accordingly, either through simple deference or through obedience to elaborate social rituals.

Dependent power comes into existence when an individual with in-dependent power, either by nature of personality or office or both, "lends" another person the right to make decisions. This can be done in three ways: (1) an individual can *grant* decision-making powers to another; (2) a group holding power can *allocate* such rights to individuals; or (3) a group or individual can *delegate* such rights to a number of other people.

Another way to look at the concept of power is to separate that which is based solely or largely on force and coercion from that which is based on group consensus. Force alone is certainly effective in the short run as a means of political control, but if it is the only basis for the people's assent to be governed, the society will be extremely rigid. Talcott Parsons once compared force in a political system to gold in a monetary system: it is effective as long as it forms a basis for other systems, but day-to-day transactions require a lesser coin if the system is not to become so rigid that it cannot adapt to new conditions (Swartz, Turner, & Tuden 1966). The Cuban revolution is a case in point. The Batista regime was so corrupt and brutal that it alienated the majority of people, including many from the upper and middle classes who would later oppose Castro as well. Since wealth was centered in a small elite and there were few methods for redressing popular grievances without threatening the system as a whole, Batista's main basis of support came from the Army. It is doubtful that Castro "won" the revolution in any military sense, since his own army never consisted of more than 2,000 men and he never succeeded in controlling a single province. But the Batista regime had become so ingrown, so self-serving, and so alienated from the populace that it virtually collapsed under the weight of its own corruption. When Batista took his money and ran, the old system lacked resilience enough to form a new government; Castro, with the only major organized force in the country, simply stepped into the power vacuum.

A government may maintain itself through force: Stalin, Idi Amin, Trujillo, Papa Doc Duvalier, Pol Pot, the British in India and Africa—twentieth-century examples are, unfortunately, legion. But if such a government is to have the flexibility to adapt to entirely new conditions, it must also possess *consensual power* which derives from the assent of the people. In state societies, such assent is not given to the wise and just alone; children, idiots, sadists, and lunatics may well be the beneficiaries of popular assent as long as they take office through established means of succession, such as being born into a kingship. Consensual power may in fact derive more from a grudging acquiescence to tradition than from respect—much less love—for those in positions of domination.

In states, consensual power is always by definition conjoined to cen-tralized control of the use of physical force, so it may be difficult to tell whether one is consenting out of respect for the system or out of fear of being thrown in jail. Would I pay my full income tax if the government did not impose physical or economic sanctions? Perhaps not. Would I voluntarily pay some part of my salary to support roads, schools, Welfare, police and fire protection, and other benefits of government even in the absence of sanctions? I like to think that I would. But I would be hard pressed to specify just how many of my tax dollars are calculated to keep me out of jail each year and how many go for support of a system which seems to provide me with certain benefits. In other words, within a state society consensual power and power by force are so intertwined that there may be something artificial in separating them for analysis. However, the distinction provides a good basis for evaluating governments both objectively and morally. Objectively, a government which possesses very little in the way of consensual power is too rigid to make the necessary adjustments to serve all its people; morally, such a government would have little justification for continued existence.

In uncentralized, egalitarian societies, leaders do not usually have access to physical coercion, but must depend entirely on consensual power. This may mean little more than setting an example. In *The Feast*, one of Napoleon Chagnon's many films on the Yanomamo Indians of Venezuela, he shows a village headman alone on his knees scraping the ground with a machete in order to shame his neighbors into helping him clean up the village compound. Similarly, during my fieldwork among the Aymara of Peru, the community mayor had to work for three days, virtually alone, on roofing a public building before others slowly began to join the labor; by the fifth day almost the entire community was involved.

In these examples the benefits of following the leader were immediately obvious, but in many cases a leader must get people to do something they do not want to do in the absence of foreseeable benefits. This may be especially true of a community leader working with a national government. The Aymara community mayor mentioned above was, on another occasion, faced with the problem of implementing a census and questionnaire for the Peruvian Ministry of Education. The people were fearful that this information would be used to tax them or to cooperativize their privately held lands, and they knew the Federal government could do nothing to punish them if they refused. The fact that they finally did assent to the questionnaire (and provided surprisingly accurate responses) suggests that they believed their mayor would use this cooperation in a long term strategy to gain benefits—roads, schools, food aid, a clinic— from the government. It is this lack of specificity about the reasons for performing an action which sharply differentiates consensual power from power based on threat, and differentiates legitimacy from coercion.

Legitimacy

Consensual power has the advantage of being free from specific sanctions and specific rewards, and it can therefore be employed in a wide variety of situations. People perform public duties because they trust either their leaders or the system the leaders represent to bring about general benefits *over the long run.* In the United States it is probably true that no individual finds every president to his liking, and many may vehemently disagree with the policies of one president or another; but few would object to a president's right to hold office. In other words, a president's *legitimacy* depends not on the continuing support of the people (indeed, polls show that at some point a majority of the people might despise a given president) but on the legal process by which that person came into office. The president draws power from the Constitution, two hundred years of history, and the belief of the American people (a belief into which they have been socialized since birth) that this particular form of government is better than the alternatives.

We might compare the situation in the United States with that of Bolivia, which at last count had undergone over 150 coups in as many years, and which at this writing is being run by a military junta devoted mainly to protecting the lucrative cocaine trade. A major reason for the instability of Bolivian governments, and for their periodic dependence on the most brutal repression to maintain power, is that there is very little basis in Bolivian society for the legitimacy of any government. In the absence of elections, kingly succession, or any evident divine guidance, one government is about as good as another, and none can claim much right to rule.

The legitimacy of power derives from the group's "political culture," the people's expectations about the nature of power and how it should be attained. For a Polynesian "big man," legitimacy may be obtained by giving the largest pig feasts; for a British king, by being born to the proper lineage; for a prime minister, by having the controlling votes of the parliament; for a nineteenth-century Cheyenne "chief," by having been brave in battle when young and being wise in age. There are cases in which legitimacy does not derive from tradition at all, but is earned in a novel manner. A dictator who comes to power through rebellion or a coup might gain legitimacy by providing benefits to his people.

Legitimacy may, moreover, have very little to do with how power is actually used. Hitler was a legitimate ruler (he became dictator through a legal loophole in the enlightened Weimar constitution); so was Stalin. Masses of people may be sustained in subjection and poverty for literally hundreds of years under legitimate governments—witness ancient Egypt and Rome, or the despotic dynasties of China. As we learn again and again from European history, a king's arbitrariness and incompetence may not deter a devoted following if his claim to the throne is legitimate. On the other hand, dictators who have no legal or traditional claim to power will almost invariably try to legitimize their positions through orchestrating demonstrations of support, staging fraudulent elections, rewriting the constitution, or creating a parliament of sycophants.

Support

Legitimacy and coercion are opposite kinds of *support*, a term which has been defined by Swartz, Turner, and Tuden (1966:10) as "anything that contributes to the formulation and/or implementation of political ends." If we consider that warring, police arrests and intimidation, striking, public speaking, voting, and simple persuasion are all encompassed in this definition, we can see that there is a continuum of supports that run the gamut from legitimacy to forceful coercion. Since support can be lost as well as gained, a government would be well advised to seek out and employ as many forms of support as possible. In analyzing a political group, we will find different supports operating in different areas and various political competitors trying to manipulate the various sources of support in their favor.

Support may be either *direct* or *indirect.* Even considering the anachronistic complexities of the electoral college, when I vote for a president in the United States, I am providing direct support. In England, however, one votes not for a prime minister but only for a representative of a certain party, so support for a given person as prime minister is once-removed, or indirect. Similarly, an African village headman may try to sway his people directly by speaking out against an opponent, or he may do so indirectly by initiating a rumor that his opponent has been indulging in witchcraft.

Process, political field, power, legitimacy, coercion, and *support* are some of the primary conceptual tools found useful by the post-structural-functionalists to analyze political systems. While these tools do not comprise a coherent philosophical school of thought, they do provide the means for analyzing a wide range of political systems.

SUGGESTED READINGS

Evans-Pritchard, E.E.
The Nuer (Oxford: Oxford University Press, 1940)
The author sets out to discover how an African pastoral group totally lacking in "government" can not only maintain continuity and cohesion but also rapidly form a united military force when necessary. His analysis is hotly argued even to this day—perhaps the highest form of compliment for one of the foundation works of political anthropology.

Fortes, M., and E.E. Evans-Pritchard (eds.)
African Political Systems (Oxford: Oxford University Press, 1940)
This is the book that started it all. The eight ethnographic studies, all by Big Men of British anthropology, represent the high standards of fieldwork already attained during the 1930s. Special mention might be made of Max Gluckman's contribution on the Zulu (which already reveals the seeds of his later rebellion against structural-functionalism) and Evans-Pritchard's highly compressed summary of Nuer political organization.

Gluckman, Max
Custom and Conflict in Africa (New York: Barnes and Noble, 1956)
The titles of the chapters—"The Peace in the Feud," "The Frailty in Authority," "The License in Ritual," for example—give a good idea of the author's fondness for paradox. Gluckman, founder of the "Manchester School" of social anthropology, believed that constant tension and conflict created a rough equilibrium. Although some writings from this period might now be relegated to the status of historical curiosities, Gluckman remains a jolly good read.

Swartz, Marc J., Victor Turner, and Arthur Tuden (eds.)
Political Anthropology (Chicago: Aldine, 1966)
The introduction to this book provides the basic philosophy and model for the "process approach," and the book as a whole is a virtual manifesto against structural-functionalism. The articles are too diverse to fit neatly into the categories provided by the editors, but many of them are of high quality. Of special mention: Ralph Nicholas's "Segmentary Factional Political Systems," Ronald Cohen's "Power, Authority, and Personal Success in Islam and Bornu," and John Middleton's "The Resolution of Conflict among the Lugbara of Uganda."

Power among the Kwakiutl of the Northwest Coast is highly individual and is attained through a manipulation of cultural expectations, including the garnering of expensive copper shields (Smithsonian Institution, National Anthropological Archives, Bureau of American Ethnology Collection).

CHAPTER 7

The Individual in the Political Arena

Two quite different lines of inquiry are implicit in the process approach. On the one hand, the breakdown of the domination of structural-functionalism freed anthropologists to widen the scope of their study of relatively uniform tribal societies to include complex nation-states. On the other hand, researchers could also shift their focus from the broad structural view of whole systems to the actions of individuals operating within those systems. The latter orientation came to be called "action theory," a term derived from German sociologist Max Weber and applied to political anthropology by Abner Cohen (1974:40–43).

As is true with so many "theories," action theory was developed *ex post facto* by seeking out the common denominator of a wide variety of studies by authors who probably had little conception that they were part of a coherent new orientation. That common denominator was the focus on individuals and their manipulative strategies to gain and maintain power. The individual involved in this process might be a named person, described with as much depth of characterization as one would find in a good novel, or he might be an abstraction: Political Man. In contrast to his close cousin Economic Man, Political Man does not maximize wealth or profit, but rather *power*. Place two or more of these beings in the same arena (which is redundant, since it is their presence which in fact creates a political arena) and we have the personae for a *social drama* or, if one prefers, for a *game* in which various moves are restricted by rules and in which there can be but one winner at a time.

In this microcosmic setting the crucial concepts include goal orientation, manipulative strategies, manoeuvring, and decision making. But individuals can never act alone in politics; they must seek followers, make alliances, and interact with other individuals in positions of either dominance or subordination. It is therefore impossible for anyone who studies politics to ignore groups. But action theorists tend to look at groups from the point of view of individuals and to emphasize groups—such as factions, cliques, and elites—which can best be understood in terms of face-to-face interactions.

The Social Drama

One of the earliest studies to develop this orientation (and already a major contender for the status of anthropological classic) is Victor Turner's *Schism and Continuity in an African Society* (1957). Though in the line of Max Gluckman's Manchester School of anthropological theory, this work had several aspects that were unique. Instead of examining the whole group of the Ndembu of northern Rhodesia, Turner focuses on individuals as they pass through a series of crises (in Turner's words, "social dramas"). Each of these dramas is analyzed as the culmination of a long period of building tensions in which new power alignments and shifts of allegiance have been taking place.

For Turner, "the widest community of Ndembu is . . . a community of suffering"; and indeed his central antagonist, Sandombu, is a true tragic hero. In the first of a complex series of social dramas involving this man, who has ambitions to be headman of Mukanza village, Sandombu twice insults the village headman, Kahali, as a challenge to his authority. This results in a fierce dispute between them, each threatening the other with sorcery. Sandombu leaves for another village where a notorious sorcerer is supposed to live. A short time later, the insulted headman falls sick and dies. Sandombu is allowed to return to Mukanza, but there is sufficient suspicion to prevent him from replacing the headman, and a man from another lineage is chosen.

This train of events is deceptively simple. Sandombu's insult to Kahali was a breach of one of the deepest principles of Ndembu social organization—the authority of the elder generation over the younger. Furthermore, Sandombu was Kahali's sister's son, and succession from older to younger within the same lineage was looked on with disfavor. There were other reasons to put a check on Sandombu's ambitions. He was sterile and his sister was barren. This, in itself a sign of sorcery, had important implications: since the Ndembu are matrilineal and a leader must draw his strength from his kinsmen through the female line, the sister's lack of children would narrow Sandombu's basis of support. Also, his indiscriminate generosity—a function of his ambition—had brought in strangers who were threatening to the conservative villagers. Finally, rivals for headmanship had an obvious vested interest in accusing Sandombu of sorcery. The result was that the village's three most powerful lineages united in opposition to Sandombu.

For Turner, the norms and structures which had so interested the generation of the 1940s have become the social field, the background before which the real action takes place. Lineage systems, marriage rules, values, and behavioral norms are not unalterable realities but social idealizations subject to constant manipulation. For example, the norm regarding succession within the lineage was applied to Sandombu but not to Kosanda, who later succeeded his mother's brother as headman. Accusations of sorcery were used to justify public consensus that Sandombu should not be headman; they were only secondarily the basis for such consensus. Thus norms and rules were not abjectly followed but were emphasized or de-emphasized according to a complex set of criteria.

Such an approach rests on certain underlying assumptions about the nature of society. Society is viewed as a "field of forces" in dynamic tension in which centrifugal and centripetal tendencies constantly pull against each other. When the tension between fission and cohesiveness becomes acute, a crisis develops, climaxing in the reestablishment of a temporary and unstable equilibrium. There is seldom a complete resolution of tensions; rather, the result is a readjustment of forces that lends more strength to one side and depletes the strength of the other. Turner, along with Marc Swartz and Arthur Tuden (1966) has elaborated this process into a diachronic model of "political phase development" in which a period of "mobilization of political capital" is followed by an encounter or "showdown." The latter involves some sort of breach of the peace in which one party in the conflict attempts to openly challenge the other. This leads to a crisis—"a momentous juncture or turning point in the relations between components of a political field"—which in turn brings about counteracting tendencies as the social group marshalls peacemaking forces to avoid complete cleavage of the two sides. "Deployment of adjustive or redressive mechanisms" may involve informal arbitration, legal machinery, or public ritual. Finally, there will be a restoration of the peace as the two parties either readjust to a new set of asymmetric power relations, or schism entirely.

Though Turner's book was transitional and still grounded in the structural-functionalism of the 1940s (his stated goal was "to isolate the cardinal factors underlying Ndembu residential structure"), many of the ideas that would later coalesce as action theory were already evident. In Sandombu we see Political Man as a real-life individual, manipulating cultural rules, making choices, developing strategies—in short, making goal-oriented decisions.

A major reason for focusing on individuals rather than on groups is that in the individual a number of different systems meet. A group may act out a single role at a particular time, but the individual always embodies conflicting roles, at once father and son, leader and follower, warrior and peacemaker. The individual thus expresses the contradictions that may be invisible in studies of groups.

Game Theory

An interesting and influential variation of action theory is the non-mathematical game theory developed by F.G. Bailey in *Stratagems and Spoils* (1969). Since this is one of the more comprehensive anthropological political analyses, it is worth reviewing in some detail. Bailey started this book after he became fascinated by the revelations emerging from the television interrogations of Mafia informer Joseph Valachi. These revealed not only a rational structure underlying organized crime but also a set of "rules of the game" by which mobsters fought and murdered one another in ongoing power struggles. Processes of leadership succession seemed to be nearly identical to those described by Frederick Barth (1959) in his game-theory analysis of the Swat Pathans of Pakistan. It seemed that "the edge of anarchy is fenced off with rules," that no matter how amorphous a political system may be, political combat is regulated by a code of which the participants may or may not be consciously aware. Each culture develops its own set of these rules of political manipulation. It is therefore possible to view politics as a "competitive game" with agreed-on rules and, equally important, an agreed-on goal. In a real sense politics *is* this set of rules, for a struggle in which each party could make up rules along the way would be simply a "fight." There are two types of political game rules: *normative rules* which are publicly professed, usually vague (honesty, sportsmanship, etc.), and according to which actions may be judged ethically right or wrong; and *pragmatic rules*, which have to do with the actual winning of the game, as opposed to public display. Bailey focuses on the latter, because the real question, as he sees it, is not whether an action is publicly approved, but whether it is effective.

The competition takes place within a *political field*, which may be defined as a society or segment of society in which two or more rival political structures exist, but in which there is an absence of an agreed-on set of rules between these structures. Within the political field are *arenas* where *teams* that accept such rules attempt to build support for themselves and to undermine their opponents through subversion. Competition may not be confined to an arena but may move from one arena to another within the wider political field, and sometimes competitive groups within an arena might unite temporarily against an outside threat.

There are five major elements of political structure when it is viewed as a game. First there must be *prizes or goals*, which are culturally defined and must be sufficiently valued by the participants to make competition meaningful. Second are the *personnel* involved in the conflict: this includes the entire concerned political community, the political elite (those entitled to compete) and the political teams involved in competition. The third element is *leadership*, which includes the individuals supported by a group of followers, on the one hand, and those individuals who actually make decisions and settle disputes, and who may be quite different from the overt leadership, on the other. Fourth is the *competition* itself, which is of two types: confrontation, or a move within the political arena that announces to an opponent one's strength in resources and one's possible intentions; and encounter, in which both contestants publicly agree to test their strength against each other. Finally, there are *judges*, who define the rules to be followed when one or another of the opponents breaks the rules.

Broadly speaking, there are two types of political team: contract and moral. A *contract team* is one that is united, not by conscience, but by the profit or potential profit to be derived from following a certain leader. A relatively loose form of contract team is the *transactional team*, which is based largely on interchanges of a material nature—money, food, clothing, contracts, licenses—so that the bond between leaders and followers is based strictly on perceived material benefit. In "big man" systems, such as those found in Polynesia, the leader must buy loyalty through loans and feasting. In factions similar to a labor union, the leader's power may depend upon his subordinates' perception that he can gain them more pay and benefits than his competitors within the movement. Since a leader's position may be based upon face-to-face transactions with individual followers, and since a leader would be well advised to avoid sharing his power for fear of creating a rival, such teams are extremely limited in size. The *bureaucratic team*, another form of contract team, avoids some of these difficulties. Here, leadership is allocated to a number of different functionaries, each with a specialized place in the hierarchy of power, so the core leader can avoid any direct challenge by duplicating his own power. Such a group also has the advantage of being able to expand indefinitely, since it does not depend on personal interactions with one individual.

In contrast to teams in which loyalties depend on personal benefits, a *moral team* will be united by a shared ethic—religious belief, nationalism, or a utopian political ideology. A leader in such a team pays the price of being rigidly confined within the normative values of the group, but a certain sense of security may also be derived from the knowledge that his followers will not shift to one who can offer better material benefits. The leader of a moral team may claim a monopoly on certain mystical attributes, such as access to the gods, which will effectively cut off opposition. For example, among the Lugbara of Uganda only the elders can use the power of the ancestor spirits—a fact which prevents the younger generation from ever seriously challenging the elders' authority.

Whatever the type of team, a leader must fulfill certain functions: decision making, recruitment and maintenance of the group, and interaction with the world outside the team. Day-to-day decision making will follow the lines of normative or pragmatic rules, or a combination of both, so that real leadership is called for only in conditions of uncertainty.

In making decisions, the leader must always calculate the political expense, especially when normative rules cannot be routinely applied. The safest strategy in such cases is for the leader to make the decision which requires the smallest social adjustment possible. The least expensive decision will be consensual; that is, the leader gains prior consent and simply announces the decision of the group. But attaining such consensus can be a long, difficult, and divisive process and might even suggest weakness in the leader. The most politically expensive form of decision making is simple command. The leader who knows the game would, of course, seek that middle ground in which he could assert power while maintaining maximum support.

While Bailey emphasizes rules as essential to the game of politics, he notes that outright cheating or playing one set of rules against another are also part of the game. In the Watergate scandal (an example Bailey could not have foreseen in 1969), pragmatic and normative rules came into conflict. Spying on opponents has long been part of American party politics, and might even be considered legitimate within the pragmatic rules. But such behavior must be kept out of sight. When the attempted bugging of the Democratic headquarters surfaced, a Pandora's box of purely pragmatic actions emerged with it—an enemies list, "dirty tricks" played on Democratic candidates, tampering with evidence, a cover-up conspiracy, and the like. None of this should have been particularly surprising to American voters, who as a group are fairly well imbued with a healthy cynicism toward politics. Perhaps even more damaging than the actual crimes was the revelation in the Watergate tapes of the appallingly petty and downright sleazy manner in which the most powerful men on earth were conducting business. With Nixon's resignation and the criminal conviction of his aides, normative values temporarily triumphed over pragmatic politics, even creating the temporary illusion that a government could be conducted by normative rules (Jimmy Carter ran for election on the basis of his high morality and promise that he would never lie to the public). At this writing, everything seems back to normal.

Over the long run, teams which regularly compete for power must be more or less equal in strength. Periodically, however, politics in one arena will spill over into another, larger arena in which one team will find itself *encapsulated* by a much larger political structure; neither the normative nor the pragmatic rules of either group will apply to the other. Three types of relations are possible in such cases. First, the larger structure may maintain only the most nominal relations with the smaller, especially if the cultures of the two groups are markedly different and the smaller group maintains a significant degree of power within its limited domain. During the colonial period in India, for example, there were large areas on the borders of China and Burma which were ignored by the British overlords except for paramilitary tours of inspection to maintain an illusion of control (however, British normative values were so offended by the practices of human sacrifice and infanticide among these people that they ultimately fought a twenty-year war to subdue them). A second alternative is predatory encapsulation. At its most primitive, this is simply a national form of the gangster protection racket: as long as the weaker group pays its tribute, it will be left alone. A more sophisticated version is the indirect rule elevated to an art by the British in Africa. Finally, the smaller group may be incorporated into the larger, through either radical change or abolition of the indigenous political, economic, and social structures. This has been tried periodically with the American Indians through processes of forced detribalization; but it has failed because the values of the dominant and the subordinate groups have differed too radically for such incorporation to take place.

Whatever the process of encapsulation, *middlemen* will assume an important political role in mediating between the two structures. The success of a middleman depends on his ability to deceive, since a compromise will usually be possible only if each side is misrepresented to the other. As a result, these middlemen will be despised by both sides. This is evident, for example, in the use of the term *cholo*, which has a derogatory connotation, for an intermediary class of Indians who are between the peasants and the *mestizos* in highland Peru and Bolivia. *Cholos* are Indians who have left the land for jobs in trucking, contraband, and small-market sales, and who prefer to speak Spanish and dress in *mestizo*-style clothes. Though distrusted by the peasants—who consider them exploitive—and despised by the *mestizos*, *cholos* fulfill an important function in bridging two radically different cultures during a period of rapid acculturation.

The problem facing any encapsulated political structure is one of survival—how to maintain itself with a minimum of change within its changed environment. A moral team, especially one based on a religious ideology, might assume the fanatic's stance and vow to fight to the last man, woman, and child. Unfortunately, the more powerful group may be thoroughly unimpressed, in which case the encapsulated group will find itself forced to change. Bailey isolates three types of political change. *Repetitive change*, so well described by Max Gluckman (1960, 1969), is quite radical change that can take place within a wider equilibrium. All groups, for example, must face the problems of losing a leader and finding a replacement, of periodic war, of famine, and so forth. In such cases, normative rules and pragmatic rules, such as rules of succession, will be sufficient to bring the society back to normal. While repetitive change has no cumulative element—small changes do not necessarily add up to a fundamental change of structure—in *adaptive change* there can be no return to the original equilibrium. In this case, normative rules can be maintained, but the pragmatic rules will have to change to account for new conditions. For example, when Plains Indian tribes were forced onto reservations, they were able to maintain most of their original culture and political values, even though their political situation had shifted from one of autonomy to one of abject dependence. In cases of *radical change*, both normative and pragmatic rules are irrevocably altered—the Russian Revolution, for example, or the independence of the British colonies after World War II.

Factions

One of the direct outgrowths of the process approach in the late 1950s was an increasing focus on the role of temporary political conflict groups or "factions." As long as equilibrium was considered the goal of social organization, factions were viewed as maladaptive. From the point of view of process theory, however, it was evident that in certain circumstances factions could be more adaptive than conventional politics in organizing and channeling political conflict, especially during periods of rapid social change. Factionalism could even comprise the permanent politics of a group. So useful was the concept that Edwin Winkler (1970:333) proclaimed the concept of faction as "perhaps the most distinctively anthropological approach to the study of inputs to a political system." It was factionalism, in Winkler's view, that had refocused anthropology from its structural obsessions to a concern with how structural principles are manipulated. Naturally such enthusiasm required dampening. Janet Bujra (1973:132) protests that factions and factionalism "are fashionable concepts enjoying a vogue which outstrips their present clarity of usage," and so-called theories of factions are little more than attempts to define the concept in a way that is relevant to a particular society. In any case, "faction" seems firmly established in the anthropologist's lexicon and so must ultimately face the same barrage of criticism as terms like "tribe" or "segmentary lineage."

In contrast to ongoing corporate groups with fixed structural properties—such as political parties, lineages, clans, or secret societies—factions tend to be informal, spontaneous, leader-follower groups organized for a particular purpose and disbanding when that purpose is accomplished or defeated. They are primarily conflict groups organized in opposition to one or more other groups; thus by definition there can never be only one faction in a specific political arena. Since a faction leader draws support from any and all available sources, his following may cross-cut normal party, class, or caste lines, with the result that there is often a lack of ideological focus.

Within this broad definition, a number of different types of factions may be delineated. Common-parlance "factionalism" refers to temporary conflicts within formal political groups, for instance, within the Republican party before a national convention. By contrast, *pervasive factionalism* develops when external pressures cause the breakdown of normal political mechanisms. In such circumstances, unorganized and temporary factions may arise with little provocation (Siegal and Beals 1970). The term *segmentary factional political system* has been applied to groups in which factions constitute the dominant mode of political organization. An example in Govindapur village in India is the Potter caste group, which, though cohesive, is not large enough to act as an effective political unit. It therefore serves its own interests by regularly aligning with one or another of the factions of the dominant caste. As with pervasive factionalism, this type is usually found in systems undergoing rapid change, where rules of political conflict have become ambiguous (Nicholas 1965, 1966). On the other hand, types of political systems which are relatively stable may have factionalism as a virtually institutionalized form of decision making. This would be true, for example, of the Ndembu or of modern Japanese government with its myriad fluctuating political "parties."

Since factions are born and nourished in conflict, they cannot reach a point of even relative equilibrium and still maintain their status as factions. There are four possibilities. first a faction may so decisively defeat its rival that it becomes legitimized and begins to organize itself as a formal group, while the defeated faction disappears altogether. Second, in states where there is only one legitimate political party, as in Communist countries, factionalism may simply serve the functions of party politics. A third possibility is that factions within an arena may continue over time with neither side winning a victory, so that conflict itself becomes increasingly ritualized and gamelike. Finally, factions may be institutionalized as political parties (Bujra 1973).

Political Symbolism

For Abner Cohen (1979), one of the most prolific of all political anthropologists, man is fundamentally "two-dimensional": he is both Man-the-Symbolist and Man-the-Political-Being, and these two functions are in constant and inseparable interaction. Politics is defined as "the distribution, maintenance, and exercise of the struggle for power within a social unit." Power itself is no less than what is expressed in any relation of domination and subordination, and is therefore an aspect of *all* social relationships. To think of power in terms of physical force or coercion is to miss entirely the subtlety with which it is usually manifested, for in day-to-day transactions power is "objectified, developed, maintained, expressed or camouflaged" by means of symbolism. All symbolism—or virtually all—has a political component.

Directly political symbolism is more sign than symbol, and therefore is not particularly effective. A blatantly political speech may be immediately effective, but it is incapable of further elaboration or manipulation; the funeral of a statesman, on the other hand, resonates with meaning— a reaffirmation of cultural values, ideas of continuity and rebirth, and much more. Politics is thus most powerfully manifested in overtly nonpolitical institutions like kinship, marriage, other rites of passage, ethnicity, elitism, and various group ceremonies.

If symbolism is virtually synonymous with "culture," and if all symbolism is political, one might suspect that Cohen has postulated that "political anthropology is nothing other than social anthropology brought up to a high degree of abstraction." This is, in fact, a direct quote from

Cohen (1979:81)—one for which he admits to having been widely criticized. Symbolism and politics would seem to be such wide-ranging concepts that they lose meaning, almost as though one were to resort to "God" as a primary element in scientific explanation. If this were truly so, Cohen would rate no more attention from his colleagues than "scientific creationists" rate from evolutionary biologists. Fortunately, however, Cohen is quite capable of bringing these abstractions down to earth, defining them precisely, and demonstrating their application in specific incidents, as he has done in some of the most insightful political ethnographies yet written.

All symbolism is *bivocal*—it serves both existential and political ends. It is existential in the sense that it relates to personal development through integrating the individual personality and relating that individual to his group. A painful puberty initiation ritual involving circumcision, for example, will be a powerful personal experience in which the child feels that he is in some way transformed, that his old self has been obliterated and a new, more adaptive self reborn in its place. At the same time, the ritual will be an opportunity for a lineage to come together to reaffirm its unity, for the mythology of origin to be reiterated, for decisions to be made, for leaders to present themselves, and for males to reaffirm their moral and physical domination over females, elders over young, and wise over merely strong. Though symbolism is largely unconscious, and is virtually constant in every person's life, its political component is most clearly manifested in the compressed dramas of ritual and ceremony. A study of these within any particular group will reveal the location of power as well as how it is manipulated. In this sense, Cohen is elaborating upon the ideas of Max Gluckman and Victor Turner, as well as the "symbolic transactionalist" school of political sociology.

In *The Politics of Elite Culture* (1981), Cohen applies these general concepts to politics in a small African nation. Sierra Leone is a nation state of about 2.5 million people, of which something less than 2 percent— nearly all of whom live in the capital, Freetown—are Creoles who view themselves as the descendents of slaves emancipated by the British. They are not an ethnic group, a tribal group, or a "class" (many non-Creoles share the same economic status), and their relation to slave-ancestors is partly mythical, since their kinship system is sufficiently open that many have been incorporated who can make no claims to special ancestry. They possess virtually no executive power in the state, lack any access to physical force, and have only the most negligible role as businessmen or producers of tangible goods.

Yet the Creoles are not only a closely-knit, on-going group, they also control enormous political power within Sierra Leone. To understand how they have accomplished this, Cohen examines the manner in which symbolism is used to create the "mystique of eliteness" and to legitimize that mystique outside their own ranks so that others will accept their claim to power.

Elitism is a way of life. People outside the group can be trained, through schooling or apprenticeship, in the technical and administrative skills necessary for government, but one can join the elite only through undergoing a long period of socialization. Elitism derives not from wealth or specific social functions, but from a vast and complex body of symbols including manners, styles of dress, accent, recreational activities, rituals, ceremonies, and a host of other traits. Skills and abilities which can be taught are conscious, while that great body of symbols that form true elitism are, by and large, unconscious.

Such symbols must serve a dual purpose: they must be at once particularistic, serving to unite the group and maintain its unique identity, and universalistic, legitimizing it as an agency of power to the great majority of outsiders.

The continuing existence of the Creoles as a separate group is constantly threatened. Most Creole wealth rests upon property ownership in Freetown and vicinity, and rising property values have created a strong temptation to sell to outsiders. In addition, a former power base in the civil service has been eroded as educated provincials compete for these positions. While Creoles comprise 64 percent of all professionals—dominating the judiciary, medicine, teaching, and the clergy—they have already lost the niche they once held in business. To counter these challenges, the once loosely-knit Creole elite has had to create more formalized institutions and more intensive means of communication, and to increasingly emphasize ceremony and ritual.

Women have always played a primary role in maintaining Creole separateness, mainly through the socialization of children in group symbols and values, and through the socialization of men in proper decorum. Equally important, women are the center of both family and kin networks (as men are more preoccupied with careers and male clubs) and are thus the pillars of a Grand Cousinhood which forms the underlying structure for the Creoles as a corporate group. This cousinhood involves dense networks of overlapping families, uniting each individual to many different families through participation in various ceremonials.

For men, Freemasonry provides an important means of group maintenance and a system of interpersonal communication. While Freemasonry is not limited to Creoles, they comprise the majority of the seventeen Masonic Lodges in Freetown, and hold most of the upper positions. Frequent ceremonies, often of a costly nature, formalize and cement group relations, while an enforced system of "brotherhood" encourages the amicable settlement of misunderstandings among individuals. Freemasonry thus provides the setting for a group identity among men, and for individual face-to-face interaction.

All of these institutions not only serve the particularistic ends of group maintenance, but also universalistic ends oriented toward the wider public. Women are involved in running a variety of associations, societies, clubs, and activities that are either partially or wholly devoted to public welfare. The Freemasons are also involved in public works projects; but more importantly, the Masonic Brotherhood provides a setting for wheeling-and-dealing and exchange of information among men who are responsible, either directly or indirectly, for national policy decisions. Thus the same sets of institutions and symbols that unite the Creoles into a closed group legitimize them as spokespersons for the public good.

This is true also of the various ceremonies and rituals that emerge from the five "cults" of the Creoles: the cults of the dead and of the Church, of Freemasonry, family, and decorum. Funerals, thanksgiving rituals, Masonic initiations, balls, marriages, and other social events are carefully orchestrated *dramas*, tightly defined and intensely meaningful actions set apart from the aimless meandering of the normal flow of daily life. Through such drama private experience, such as marriage or the death of a loved one, is elevated to collective experience. For all participants, dramas are intensely tangible and immediate, but at the same time they connect the individual and group with the timeless motifs of male and female union, victory and defeat, life and death. At every point, then, the acted symbol unites the immediate and the timeless, the individual and the collective, the parochial and the national, the selfish and the giving, the private and the public.

Although it was Cohen who was most responsible for introducing the term "action theory" into political anthropology, it is debatable whether his symbolic approach should be so classified. He does not analyze individual action, except to provide examples for more general processes, and he is emphatic that individual decision making must not be unduly snatched from its cultural context to give an illusion of more freedom than really exists. On the other hand, it is perhaps Cohen more than any other who has broadened the scope of action theory by clarifying the *symbolic field* within which individuals act and which provides both the constraints and the raw materials for those striving for power.

SUGGESTED READINGS

Bailey, F.G.
Strategems and Spoils (New York: Schocken Books, 1969)
Bailey's theory (summarized in the foregoing chapter) provides one of the few systematic models in anthropology for analyzing political systems. One important aspect of the theory is the explicit differentiation between the ideal political system and the real political system.

Barth, Frederick
Political Leadership among the Swat Pathans (London: Athalone Press, 1959)
"In Swat, persons find their place in the political order through a series of choices." This simple observation and his supporting analysis placed Barth in the forefront of the reaction against purely structural studies that ignored individual decision making. As a result, this book and several journal articles on the Pathans of the Swat Valley in Afghanistan became the basis for Bailey's political game theory.

Cohen, Abner
Two-Dimensional Man (Berkeley: University of California Press, 1976)
For Cohen, Man-the-Symbolist and Man-the-Politician are complementary and mutually reinforcing. In this work Cohen presents his theory of the dialectical relationship between power and symbolism. The argument tends to become abstract, so it helps to read it in concert with one of Cohen's excellent ethnographic studies, such as *The Politics of Elite Culture* or *Custom and Politics in Urban Africa*.

Cohen, Abner
The Politics of Elite Culture (Berkeley: University of California Press, 1981)
Cohen is at his best when applying his concepts of power and symbolism in the analysis of a specific group. This book is one of very few studies of a power elite that is based on participant observation fieldwork. Though the subjects are the Creoles of Sierra Leone, one feels that this could just as well be a study of a United States elite.

Fogelson, Raymond D., and Richard N. Adams (eds.)
The Anthropology of Power (New York: Academic Press, 1977)
"Power" is defined in an extremely broad (and not always political) sense in order to provide a common thread to tie together these 26 ethnographic studies and four theoretical articles. Of the latter, Richard Adams's evolutionary model of

power is a significant contribution. One will also find excellent analyses of the concepts of *mana* in the South Pacific, *Wakan* among the Sioux, and shamanism among the Northwest Coast Indians.

Turner, Victor W.
Schism and Continuity in an African Society (Manchester: Manchester University Press, 1957)
There are few books in political anthropology that deserve the status of classic; this is one of them. In many ways, this minute examination of power struggles within a single village of the Ndembu of northern Rhodesia is reminiscent of Chinua Achebe's famous novel *Things Fall Apart;* here also we find the tragic overreacher, barred from the status and power he so desperately desires. In spite of Turner's scholarly presentation, Sandombu comes to life. The methodology is the case study or "social drama," in which a few specific events are examined in detail.

Even the Congress of the United States is no longer beyond the scrutiny of anthropologists (Library of Congress).

CHAPTER 8

Politics in Industrial Society

Nowhere has the line between political anthropology and political sociology become more blurred than in the studies of modernization and the formal political institutions of industrial society. Anthropology has been characterized traditionally by its subject matter—*informal political* structures in relatively closed preindustrial societies—and by its emphasis on participant observation as the primary method of research. Recently, however, anthropologists have increasingly turned their attention to the political integration (or nonintegration) of tribal groups in developing nations, and to such formal political structures as parties, governmental bureaucracies, and even multinational corporations. In such contexts, it may be impossible to gather information by immersing oneself in the culture. Indeed, a national political party may crosscut any number of cultural divisions, so that interviewing, questionnaires, and the study of documents may be the most useful techniques of research. While one can buy one's way into a Yanomamo village with a few machetes, the vice president of a multinational corporation might be less amenable to such inducements, with the result that access to even the most basic information may be tightly restricted. Though the anthropologist is freed from the threat of hepatitis or of having to eat grubs, he faces an entirely new set of problems and must choose his research according to the availability of information. One result is that the growing number of anthropological

117

studies of modern political systems, while individually of high quality, seem catch-as-catch-can when viewed as a group.

Despite this lack of a theoretical common denominator, such studies usually do retain a distinctly anthropological flavor. Politics is not treated as analytically separate, but rather as embedded in a wider culture. Small segments, modern equivalents of the band or the tribal village, are investigated as representing the whole. The informal mechanisms that underlie formal organization are emphasized.

Processes Of Modernization

Until about a decade ago, both common sense and "scientific" ideas of modernization coincided. As articulated by W.W. Rostow (1960), the process could be divided into five stages. First came traditional society, characterized economically by a low level of technology, a high concentration of resources in agriculture, and a low ceiling on productivity. In the second stage the basic preconditions for development are set: an effective centralized national state and the spread of the belief in economic progress. During this transition period capital is mobilized, trade increases, technology develops, and the government begins to support economic growth. At a certain threshold, "take-off" occurs—the society kicks into high gear. From there it will "drive to maturity" (stage 4) of its own momentum until stage 5, an "age of high mass-consumption" (maturity?), is reached.

All this might sound vaguely familiar to anthropologists who recall nineteenth-century theories that postulated a unilineal social evolution leading from savagery to barbarism to civilization, or from animism to polytheism to monotheism (with the process usually culminating in the great civilization of imperial Anglican England, since most of the writers were British). In retrospect it all seems like harmless, if slightly ethnocentric, fun—until we remember that related ideas under the misnomer of Social Darwinism provided the philosophical justification for monopoly capitalism and all the horrors of early industrialization. In a similar manner, the Stages of Growth theory has provided the West with the rationalization for unmitigated economic imperialism.

In a series of articles and books, S.N. Eisenstadt (a political sociologist adopted by anthropology) has developed an alternative model of Third World modernization. The unilineal model favored by every United States administration up to the present is applicable only to Western Europe and the United States in their initial phases. Third World countries reveal a remarkable variety of development patterns, some absolutely contradictory to the "stages" theory. For example, there is often a *negative* correlation between the degree of industrial development and literacy, mass media, education, and the like; in many countries development is so concentrated that only a handful of the population share its benefits, while the living conditions of the vast majority actually deteriorate (we find this in Guatemala, Nicaragua under Somoza, and to a lesser extent, Brazil). Similarly, it was widely held that modernization required the breakdown of traditional inherited institutions, such as tribalism or kinship groups, whereas in many countries the maintenance of such groups is integral to economic development; disruption of such institutions is as likely to lead to disorganization and chaos as to modernization. Finally, virtually no Third World country has attained "take-off," in the sense of industrial growth involving the majority of the population.

Recent theorists have tended to stress either internal or external factors in modernization, though these two emphases are not incompatible. First, modernization may be analyzed as an unfolding of inherent traditional structures—tribes, lineages, ethnic groups, secret societies, etc.—which may change functions and goals while actually increasing their cultural cohesiveness. We have already seen an example of this in Cohen's analysis of the Creole elite of Sierre Leone. It is also possible to focus on relations of dependency and exploitation, that is, on the imperialism and colonialism stemming from Western capitalist expansion.

According to Eisenstadt, the "common core" of modernization is *social differentiation* and *social mobilization*. The political sphere must be sufficiently differentiated from the religious sphere if the society is to be flexible enough to make the adjustments necessary to the constant change that is integral to the modernization process. In both prerevolutionary China and the Islamic countries, modernization has been severely retarded because of the identity of conservative religious tradition with politics. "Social mobilization" refers to the process by which traditional social and psychological loyalties are broken down so that new rearrangements of society and economy may become possible. This does not mean that traditional structures cease to exist or that anomie is a necessary concomitant to modernization; rather, traditional groups may simply restructure themselves or reorient old structures toward new goals.

In relation to politics specifically, administrative centralization and political elites are crucial elements of the modernization process. Centralization requires, first of all, an ideological transformation in which at least some local loyalties are shifted to a national government, or, more likely, one in which traditional groups begin to perceive the benefits accruing to them through support of a national government. This of course requires establishment symbols—flags, national heroes, national origin myths, national-level enemies—which are flexible enough to relate many diverse groups to the center. Centralized government, which requires some sort of bureaucratic framework, calls forth new organs of political competition (such as factions, special interest groups, and political parties) which must develop new rules of the political game. These rules can range from democratic voting to the Bolivian-style coup. Modernization invariably begins with some sort of elite center—rich landowners, an entrepreneurial class, or the military. All too often, both economic and political modernization will be restricted to this core group, resulting in a situation of *internal colonialism* in which a few small elites centered in one city exploit the rest of the country. In such "patrimonial states," common to Southeast Asia and Latin America, the elitist monopoly on modernization and political process is established as a permanent condition. If modernization is to expand beyond these elites, it proceeds through ever-widening political socialization as new groups and new strata of society are brought into the political process.

Political Ethnicity and Retribalization: The Hausa Case

It is often contended that modernization leads to ethnic uniformity. Ostensibly, old tribal loyalties are shifted to the centralized nation-state, and politics itself becomes detribalized in the sense that factions and parties cross-cut local and ethnic divisions. In *Custom and Politics in Urban Africa* (1969), Abner Cohen shows that the case may be just the opposite; modernization may lead to a reformation and hardening of ethnic identity.

Cohen's study is of the Hausa of Nigeria—renowned traders, who have developed a widespread reputation as shrewd businessmen, exploiters, troublemakers, and geniuses at their profession. There is certain truth in at least the latter accusation, though their "genius" resides more in their trading network than in individual brilliance. The Hausa are neither pastoralists nor farmers, and therefore have had to make up in efficiency for what they lack in control over the production of the cattle and kola nuts they trade. The forest zone people of the South cannot raise their own meat because the tsetse fly kills off cattle within two weeks. The savanna people of the North put a high value on the kola nut but cannot grow this food themselves. Trading between these two ecological zones is a tricky business; since cattle die so quickly in the forest, and since the kola nut is highly perishable, one cannot simply transfer these goods from one area to another and wait around for the best price. Information on supply and demand must be obtained before goods are moved. Nor can one depend on either traders or customers having money on hand when the actual transfer is made. The Hausa trading network has solved both these technical problems: information on market conditions moves rapidly through the system, and the Hausa have established a virtual monopoly on credit and trust in these business transactions. There is nothing "primitive" or small in such trading: millions of dollars worth of goods are involved, and the wealth and income of the vast majority of the Hausa are directly or indirectly derived from the dual trading of kola and cattle. Yet despite their sophisticated knowledge of banking, insurance, and legal documents, the Hausa quite rationally prefer traditional arrangements based on partnerships of trust and reciprocity.

Cohen's study focuses on the 1962 "retribalization" of the Hausa quarter of Sabo in the city of Ibadan. Only a few decades earlier, Sabo had been little more than a Hausa sector of a largely Yoruba village; but as Ibadan grew into a major city, Hausa influence was reduced. With independence after World War II, the central government of the newly liberated nation simultaneously emphasized party politics and condemned tribalism in an attempt to unify the country. These pressures combined to weaken the effectiveness of the traditional Hausa chiefs, and both outmarriage and the revolt of the young against tribal ways threatened to detribalize the Hausa altogether. The Hausa were not particularly self-conscious nor defensive about their tribal heritage, but they became increasingly aware that their trading network, and therefore their livelihood, depended on their ethnic cohesiveness.

The Hausa answer to this political and economic challenge was to reemphasize the tribal unit. The major tool in this process was the development of a Moslem religious brotherhood called Tijaniyia. The majority of Hausa had previously, like the Yoruba, been rather casual about their religion. The Tijaniyia practiced a highly puritanical mode of religion and involved an intense form of community ritual that clearly set them off from the morally inferior non-Hausa. In addition, the Tijaniyia established a religious hierarchy that provided strong ritual leaders to fill the power vacuum left by the declining authority of the traditional chiefs. Through retribalization, Hausa ethnicity was politicized and used as a weapon in the struggle to maintain their monopoly on trade. The forces of modernization thus drove the Hausa to a degree of exclusiveness more radical than at any time in the past.

Cohen sees this tendency *away* from assimilation as a normal element in the modernization process. Indeed, *re*tribalization and *de*tribalization operate upon the same groups simultaneously: a tribal group may integrate itself at one level through increased participation in the national economy and in factional or party politics, while emphasizing its cultural distinctiveness at another level.

"Political ethnicity," or the deliberate use of ethnicity to attain political ends, should not be seen as a matter of conservatism or a striving for continuity. Old structures and traditional beliefs may be given great emphasis, but observation will reveal that their functions have changed radically.

Political Adjustment in a Reservation Context: The Mapuche

In postcolonial Africa, modernization has brought many tribal groups into national-level politics. A more common effect of modernization is that native groups lose their previous political autonomy while being barred from national politics, as has been and continues to be the case with Native Americans in the United States. Where there exists clear political, technological, and economic domination, tribal politics may have to change substantially and continually to adapt to the whims of the dominating power. Native government is faced with contradictory mandates to provide for the needs of the community while at the same time satisfying the state. One solution, chosen by some Pueblo reservations in the United States, is simply to supply nominal "chiefs" to whatever council is required by the federal government, while keeping traditional arrangements separate. This is not possible, however, where there is a great degree of dependency on national government largesse or where the national government is extremely intrusive. L.C.Faron's (1967) ethnohistoric account of the Mapuche of Chile reveals tribal politics in an almost constant process of change in response to the varying policies of the Chilean government.

Traditionally, the Mapuche lacked any centralized political authority. The functioning social unit was the kin group, under the limited leadership of an elder called the *lonko*. During more than three hundred years of resistance to European invaders, a powerful military organization with strong war chiefs developed. By the mid-1800s, after a period of relatively peaceful defiance, the Mapuche grew increasingly restive as lands maintained through force of arms were eroded by fraudulent legal claims. Taking advantage of Chile's preoccupation with the War of the Pacific against Peru and Bolivia (1879–83), the Mapuche staged their last major uprising. They were soundly defeated, most of their lands were confiscated, and they were placed on relatively small reservations.

The Chilean government preferred to deal with each reservation through a single chief. This centralization of political authority was alien to the Mapuche, but there was sufficient precedent in the institution of strong military chiefs for a military-like power to be transferred to a peacetime office. Of course, this meant drawing power away from both the *lonkos* and the lesser military leaders. The federal government reinforced this centralization of reservation power by directly providing the chief with three times as much land as anyone else, at a time when land was a scarce and valuable commodity. Moreover, the chief was given limited legal control of all reservation land, and so many government restrictions were funnelled through him that he ended up controlling, directly or indirectly, all of the wealth of the community. Anyone wishing to set up a household within the reservation had to seek permission of the chief. This made it extremely difficult to settle disputes, as of old, by moving to another area. There was no choice but to submit to the chief. In addition, the chiefs were given responsibility for mediating Chilean law for the Bureau of Indian Affairs, and for enforcing the customary law of the Mapuche. Such a concept of centralized power depended entirely on the reservation system and on the intrusion of the federal government into native politics.

By the 1950s, the reservation chief's kingly position had become an increasing irritation to the very national government which had created it in the first place. An extremely powerful chief is in a position not only to exploit his people, but also to defend them from outside exploitation. In a deliberate attempt to break the power of these chiefs, the government began to bypass them and deal individually with the Mapuche as Chilean citizens. The predictable result was that the power of the chiefs declined almost as rapidly as it had arisen.

Some of the chief's powers reverted to the *lonkos*, whose authority nevertheless continued to be localized and traditional. With increasing interaction between the Mapuche and their wider social environment, however, and with increasing threats against their land, mediation was as necessary as ever. While the chief continued to represent the reservation (his leadership was recemented in times of real stress), a new mechanism of culture brokerage developed—the political pressure group. The *Corporación Araucana* formed to fight for maintenance of the reservations and for increased government assistance to the Indians. A smaller opposition group—the *Unión Araucana*—was conceived by the Capuchin missionaries to promote absorption of the Mapuche into Chilean society.

In sum, we find among the Mapuche a reactive and adaptive process beginning with authority vested in the elders of local kin groups, followed by the rise of war chiefs, the emergence of strong reservation chiefs, and finally by the shift of authority into the hands of political action groups.

Formal Political Institutions in Modern Society

Max Weber's now-classical studies of bureaucracy were written at a time when modern industrial organization and administration were still emerging from more personalistic forms of management. By contrast, the new systems seemed to be distinguished by cold scientific rationality, single-minded devotion to production and profit, and an almost inhuman mechanical efficiency. The nepotism and paternalism so highly valued in an earlier day gave way to a system of hiring based entirely on qualifications for specific jobs. The personal lives of workers were not to intrude into the work environment. The ideal system would seem to have been independent of individual personality altogether.

Despite vast differences in approach, the structural Durkheimian model, which displaced the Weberian model during the 1950s, presented an equally dehumanized image. Bureaucratic organizations were viewed as aggregates with structures and functions that transcended the individuals comprising them. It was sufficient to describe those structures and functions at the level of the organization itself, so that the individual worker could be virtually ignored.

Both models can still be defended, and continue to provide the theoretical basis for important studies of industrial-level organization. In fact, many of the tendencies which were merely inchoate in Weber's time have solidified, as just a glance at the flow chart of authority within a major corporation will show. Yet something is missing—the same missing element in the structural-functionalist studies of preindustrial political systems, namely, the individual. Contrary to prediction, individuals have not simply become robots in grey flannel suits within corporations. Just the opposite seems to be the case. Vine Deloria, in his book *Custer Died For Your Sins* (1969), makes the remarkable observation that corporations may ultimately turn out to be the white man's form of tribalism, a way of creating the kinds of personal face-to-face group identifications that Native Americans are trying to preserve. In any case, it requires only a slight shift of focus to see that behind the cold rationality and computerized structures are human beings who do indeed bring their lives and personalities to the job, and always have; who interact with each other in sometimes-not-entirely-rational ways; who form cliques and factions; and who are as liable to work around the formal rules as to work within them.

This of course is the stuff of which anthropology is made, and anthropologists have brought some refreshing perspectives to some hoary bureaucracies. Essentially, anthropologists have focused on two elements which have been largely ignored by political scientists: first, they have described the *informal* groups, based on class, interests, age, and education, that function within formal organizations; second, they have shown the relation between the organization, the individuals that comprise it, and the wider environment.

Bureaucracies may be described in terms of degrees of "rationality," in the Weberian sense of expressly defined goals and formal organization designed to implement these goals. A system that is rigidly rational, in which formal rules are dominant so that individual workers and administrators must act within set roles, may be successful in the short run but lack the flexibility to adapt to changing conditions. At the opposite end of the spectrum is the organization in which informal rules prevail. Here members act as individuals, not as roles or offices, and decision making is based on a wide range of personalistic relations including consultation, friendship, intimacy, factionalism, competition, and outright hostility. A third possibility, more stable than either extreme, is a balance of both formal and informal mechanisms.

A bureaucracy is not a closed system; it must constantly interact and make adaptive adjustments to its environments if it is to survive. It must compete with other organizations for scarce resources, including power. It must provide services or products that impinge on the prerogatives of others, and it must defend its own field of interest against competitors. Individuals working for the organization are also involved in external personal and professional networks that divide their time and loyalties and influence their on-job decisions.

The anthropologist, by training and through the unique role of participant-observer, is in an excellent position to describe the everyday workings of such organizations, the informal rules that guide individual behavior, and the informational networks.

Bureaucracy and Anti-Bureaucracy in Modern China

Martin King Whyte's (1980) analysis of the two faces of Communist rule in the People's Republic of China reveals how an inbuilt tendency toward rigid bureaucratic rationality can be balanced by officially sanctioned anti-bureaucratic activities.

Throughout the 1950s, China was portrayed in the West as the supreme example of bureaucratic totalitarianism. Using the Leninist-Stalinist model of socialism, Mao set out to assimilate every institution in Chinese society into one mammoth bureaucracy, organized around a highly complex system of ranks and wages. Between 1949 and 1958, the number of "state cadres" grew from 720,000 to 7,920,000 as agriculture was collectivized and powerful central bureaucracies established to control mass communications, the arts, and foreign trade. With regard to labor, the Chinese outstripped their Soviet model; virtually all labor was allocated by the state, and there were considerably more attempts to organize the after-hours activities of the workers. Bureaucratic organization even penetrated to the neighborhood and family levels of society; street committees formed in urban areas were subdivided, first into residence committees, and finally into small residence groups which jointly and separately were responsible for running local factories, for sanitation, for health, crime-prevention, and the like.

All of this was seen as necessary if a country as vast and populous as China was to function as a national unit and realize stated economic goals. Only through such means could the nation avoid duplication of effort and local group rivalries, organize labor for large scale projects, and assure some degree of equality in the distribution of goods and services.

Along with the growth of the Chinese bureaucracy, however, there developed a corresponding tendency toward anti-bureaucracy, that is, toward avoiding the negative effects of such a rigidly hierarchical scheme. In 1967, Mao himself castigated bureaucrats in general as conceited, complacent, ignorant, and endlessly competing for power and money. A major aspect of the Cultural Revolution was the disruption of the entrenched bureaucracy. Government officials must leave office periodically to purify themselves of bourgeois tendencies through manual labor or political study. There have been numerous attempts to obtain more mass input into decision making. Wall posters may even be used to expose the faults of superiors.

In addition, the Communist party itself mounts periodic campaigns to disrupt bureaucratic routine. The normal rules and procedures of administration may be denounced for hindering the enthusiasm and initiative of the masses. Central-level organizations may be moved and placed under local level authorities; even entire factories, universities, and scientific institutions have been dismantled and relocated in relatively small towns.

Whyte views such obstructions as complementary rather than contradictory to Chinese bureaucratic organization. In a society which has idealized equality, bureaucracy poses three main dangers: first, such organization inevitably creates vested interests; second, it creates a system of hierarchical ranks that threatens to coalesce into a new class to replace the overthrown capitalist class; and finally, if all power is contained in the administrative hierarchy, the ordinary worker will be disenfranchised from the decision-making process. By regularly reshuffling the bureaucracy and allowing it to be actively criticized by the masses—within limits, of course—China is able to take advantage of modern bureaucratic organization while still holding onto its revolutionary ideals.

Primitive Politics on Capitol Hill

It was perhaps inevitable that the United States Congress should fall under the anthropologist's unflinching scrutiny. As a Legislative Assistant to Senator John Glenn, anthropologist J. McIver Weatherford was perfectly placed for the participant observation research that led to his book *Tribes on The Hill* (1981). The book is popularly written and somewhat more resolutely and self-consciously anthropological in its viewpoint than may be absolutely necessary. The author perceives little difference between the United States Congress and a "primitive" tribe in terms of status rivalries, clan social structure, political socialization, and ritual. Each chapter begins with a description of some tribal practice—among the Iroquois, the Shavante of the Amazon Basin, the Kawelka of Highland New Guinea, the Aztec—which is then compared to the behavior of Congress. All this becomes somewhat perfunctory and a bit gimmicky, especially since the author is never clear when he is postulating a general principle of political behavior or using primitive tribes merely as analogies; since some of the comparisons are rather farfetched, the latter would seem to be usually the case. However, once one gets past the "pop anthropology," the author has much to say of real substance about the workings of the United States government at its highest levels. The "real" system is revealed to have only the most tenuous correspondence to the mythological civics-text system taught in high school.

A basic and universal aspect of politics is certainly the socialization of those who aspire to power. Senior senators have one absolute goal: to get reelected. Freshmen senators not only must pursue this goal against much greater odds than their elders, they must also learn the rules of the power game as it is played in Washington. The Longworth Building, where freshmen have their offices, is described as resembling the bachelor hut among some tribal groups, where young men are conditioned for their place in the social hierarchy. Before he can earn his way across the street to the Sam Rayburn Building, where senior senators reside, the freshman must build up a strong enough base of support both at home and in the Senate to get reelected a number of times. Meanwhile, he will be constantly reminded of his lowly place in the pecking order; a favorite method used by seniors to keep a freshman in place is to consistently mispronounce his name, which even the greenest senator holds to be the most sacred part of his personal mana. A freshman will be allowed short speeches on the Senate floor (usually to an empty house) and may give interviews to his home-state press without fear of being sanctioned by gossip or ostracism; but anything delivered to the national media must be extremely circumspect.

For senior senators, committee chairs may be the prime mechanism for wielding enormous power; for freshman senators, such offices are a means of creating an illusion of power for the folks back home. The committees to which the freshman has access have impressive titles: the Subcommittee on Oversight of the Internal Revenue Service; the Economic Stabilization Committee; the Western Hemisphere Subcommittee of Foreign Relations. Unfortunately (or perhaps fortunately for the public), such committees are virtually powerless. By collecting subcommittees, however, the novice will gradually build up at least a modicum of power over authorization and appropriations. Equally important, each committee and subcommittee brings new staff which can be added to the senator's clan.

Weatherford divides senators into three basic categories based on their strategies for gaining and maintaining power: shamans, warlords, and godfathers. Different strategies are adaptive to different personalities and offer different political yields.

The *shaman* is a highly visible generalist whose major function is to allay people's fears of Communism, Big Business, pollution, the Mafia, etc. Senator Edward Kennedy, the prototypal shaman, is endlessly quoted in the press and often the first on the scene (for example, during the Three Mile Island nuclear crisis, he was giving authoritative interviews before others had even established a position), though he has never gotten a significant bill passed.* The power of such men derives not from their ability to deliver results but from their skill in garnering and manipulating popular support. Other senators who fall into this category are Joseph McCarthy, Estes Kefauver, and Richard Nixon.

Warlords are those senators who try to establish a monopoly over one aspect of government and then extend that power outward to increase its scope. For example, Russell Long, as chairman of the Finance Committee, possessed a virtual monopoly on anything to do with taxation. Issues involving energy are largely in the hands of Senator Mark Hatfield, who assumed chairmanship of the Senate Appropriations Committee in 1981. Senator John Stennis of Mississippi sat on only two committees, Appropriations and Armed Services, but these were so powerful that Stennis was able to pass one of the biggest home-state boon-doggles in history as a routine inhouse operation. The Tennessee-Tombigbee Water-

---

*This example and analysis and the others in these paragraphs are all Weatherford's.

way is a $3 billion canal, longer than the Panama canal, which is parallel to and only 150 miles from the Mississippi River. Appropriations for this extravaganza, a virtual twin to the Mississippi, were passed in 1971 with few objections, since Stennis had the power to reduce or withdraw military bases in other senators' states.

In contrast to the highly visible shamans and finely focused warlords are the *godfathers,* who have mastered the art of manipulating power from behind the scenes. This is the most difficult of all roles, since it requires an exquisitely tuned sense, not only of how the system works, but also of the personal habits, fears, soft spots, and ambitions of virtually all of the members of Congress. Lyndon Johnson was the supreme godfather. At present, Speaker of the House Thomas O'Neill has assumed such a role.

Ultimately, the primary power units of Congress—virtual miniature governments within themselves—are not the individual senators and congressmen but the *clans* that form around them. The larger and more influential the clan, the greater will be its power. Clans are comparable to large kinship groups in tribal communities, and until anti-nepotism rules were established in 1967 the core of the network might be actual kin. Even today a great deal of power is concentrated through family networks. The Byrds of Virginia; the Cabots, Lodges, and Kennedys of Massachusetts; the Tafts of Ohio; and the Roosevelts of New York—all have passed their power from generation to generation, some eventually establishing family power niches (e.g., the Udalls of Utah have focused on issues of environment and natural resources) or ideological niches (Kennedy liberalism, Goldwater conservatism). Intermarriage among the various congressional families has served to ally clans and extend the networks of power.

The basic component of congressional clans is staff, but there are many ways to incorporate others. The clan network can be extended by building patron-client relations with bureaucrats who have, through the power of willful complacency, the ability to block legislation that has been enacted. Lobbies can also be incorporated into the clan network. Fifteen thousand registered lobbies and two thousand political action committees play a vital function in the government, not only in providing information on the particular issue being lobbied but also on what is going on in Congress. Congressmen may even further extend their clans by establishing their own lobbies in the form of institutes, "think tanks", or public affairs groups. Harlem congressman Adam Clayton Powell used his Tenants Protective Association, headquartered in Bimini in the Caribbean, to move large amounts of money. Senator Jesse Helms has been instrumental in the establishment of The Heritage Foundation, The Institute on Money and Inflation, The American Family Institute, The Center for a Free Society, and the Institute of American Relations.

The major thrust of Weatherford's analysis is that Congress has become so ritualized it hardly functions at all. As the Senate floor grew into a theatrical exhibition hall where impassioned rhetoric supplanted real decision making, most productive discussion and information-gathering was shifted to closed committee meetings. The Legislative Reorganization Act of 1946 not only opened these committee hearings to the public and press, but also opened them to the same kind of ritualistic showmanship as exists on the floor. As celebrities, Mafiosa, and Communists were paraded before the wise and judicious panels, however, the drama increased. Today, real decisions are made in private offices, over lunch, and in the hallways, leaving the more public arenas as showplaces for the government-as-it-should-be, that is, the government of the American myth.

The true goal of Congress, according to Weatherford, is to produce the *Congressional Record*, which is really nothing more than a repetition of the empty rhetoric displayed on the House and Senate floors, but in a form that can be mailed back home to show that the congressman is doing his job. Rules allow changes to be entered into the published version so a speech might seem more articulate than it actually was, and there is even a rule that allows entries of speeches that were never presented. Through such entries, senators can make themselves appear prime movers on certain bills, when actually they may have played no part whatsoever.

Congressmen have become so involved in ritualistic posturing—giving speeches, attending benefits, soothing constituents, and the like—that real power has shifted to the staffs who control the individual's information flow, develop resolutions and bills, and write the speeches. "The greatest deliberative body in the world has become the greatest ceremonial body in the world, and the talents of its members are devoted less to deciding matters of national policy than to arranging and considering minute points of ceremony" (Weatherford 1981:266).

Conclusions

The journey from Evans-Pritchard's *The Nuer* to Weatherford's study of the United States Congress is long and convoluted, but there is a certain logical inevitability to it. From its beginnings in relatively closed-system analyses of folk cultures, political anthropology has spread outward in every direction; there has been an increase in complexity and scope, in relation both to theory and to the societies studied. Predictably, this has led not only to greater breadth and depth in political studies, but also to increasing fragmentation. Indeed, there is little evidence that anthropologists writing on politics read each other's works; individual research often seems isolated, and there is little building on earlier studies.

Despite the wide variety of approaches, there are some significant absences. The process approach and action theory have tended toward an increasing emphasis on cognition, decision making and motivation. The materialist perspective has been left by the wayside. There are no end of analyses on how actors in political dramas manipulate symbols, rules, norms, or customs, but very little discussion is devoted to how they manipulate physical resources, or how they are affected by such resources. One of the more promising developments in social anthropology has been the application of ecological principles to show how various social forms are adaptive to changing environments; this orientation might be of great value in interpreting political behavior. Also, the trend in cultural anthropology toward increasing quantification has been largely ignored by political researchers.

With new political studies appearing regularly, it is to be expected that gaps will not remain for long. However, the crucial problem at this point is not to produce more narrowly-focused ethnographies—though these of course, are certainly valuable—but to draw together the material that already exists into some sort of cohesive framework.

The first major challenge, then, is to make political anthropology *meaningful* by incorporating the scores of isolated studies into some larger theory. The second major challenge is to make political anthropology *relevant*. In this regard, it would be a major deficiency to overlook what has come to be called "action anthropology" (to carefully distinguish it from the more benign "action theory"). It is almost inevitable that an anthropologist studying power in modern society should learn far more than he would really like to know about the effects of that power. "Oppression" is a nice word to bandy about at cocktail parties when trying to one-up a fellow liberal; it becomes a very ugly word when brought down to the level of real people suffering real hunger, real privation, and perhaps real torture and death. The emotional thresholds of individual anthropologists vary, so there is no way to determine the point at which "pure" research turns to active protest. Action anthropology is an attempt, usually futile, to confront the very powers we started studying with such illusions of objectivity and to try to redress, if only through exposure, some of the evils of modern interpretations of power. Cultural Survival, Inc., is perhaps the largest and best known of the specifically anthropological action groups; it is a combined resource center, pressure group, and communications network dedicated to the protection of traditional societies throughout the world. While such groups belong to all of anthropology, indeed to all people, political anthropologists can play a key role in exposing and analyzing systems of repression, and equally important, in developing practical recommendations for change.

Whether political anthropology will duly become cohesive and relevant to the problems of change in the modern world is a moot question, but it can no longer fall back on the excuse that it is still a fledgling discipline. Some of the finest work of modern anthropology has already been accomplished under the rubric of "political anthropology." There is certainly much to come.

SUGGESTED READINGS

Britan, Gerald M., and Ronald Cohen (eds.)
Hierarchy and Society (Philadelphia: Institute for the Study of Human Issues, 1980)
Traditionally, anthropology has tended to examine informal political structures. In this book, a score of anthropologists turn their jaundiced eyes upon formal bureaucracies only to discover that these work mainly through informal interactions. Organizations under scrutiny include a health center in the American Midwest, provincial government in Ethiopia, and the massive bureaucracy of the People's Republic of China. In a theoretical chapter, the editors summarize anthropological theory on formal organization and present their own model.

Huizer, Gerrit, and Bruce Mannhein (eds.)
The Politics of Anthropology (The Hague, Netherlands: Mouton, 1979)
Anthropologists have always considered themselves the vanguard in the fight against sexism, racism, ethnocentrism, and colonialism. It is the basic premise of this book that anthropology itself is basically sexist, racist, ethnocentric, and colonialist. The editors do not settle for mere self-accusation, however, but include articles that seriously examine the problems and possibilities of "liberation anthropology."

Seaton, S. Lee, and H.J.M. Claessen (eds.)
Political Anthropology (The Hague, Netherlands: Mouton, 1979)
This collection of papers, presented at a conference in Chicago, self-consciously attempts to present a state-of-the-art overview of its subject. It succeeds to the extent that it reveals that political anthropology remains a potpourri of unrelated theories and ethnographic analyses. The part titles—"Centers and Peripheries," "Authority and Power," and "Political Culture"—are sufficiently general to cover just about anything. Despite the lack of cohesion, many of the articles are of the highest quality. Several chapters deal with politics in industrial states.

Weatherford, J. McIver
Tribes on the Hill (New York: Rawson, Wade, 1981)
As a member of Senator John Glenn's staff, author Weatherford was able to employ participant observation research in the halls of Congress. The results (summarized in this chapter) are presented in a lively and humorous manner aimed at, and deserving, a popular audience. Though it is sometimes difficult to separate Weatherford's black humor from his scholarship, as when he compares senators to cannibals, there is no ambiguity in his main theme: Congress is so caught up in performing primitive rituals that it can barely function at all.

Glossary

Action theory A perspective within the **process approach** in which the focus is on the strategies of individuals for gaining and maintaining power.

Age-set system In some societies, all those who undergo puberty initiation at the same time form a coherent group that passes through different statuses and roles together. In tribal societies, this can be an important pantribal sodality that overrides kinship loyalties and unites the wider group.

Arena This term has no agreed-upon meaning, but in the **process approach** and **action theory** it is often used to delimit a small area within the political **field** in which competition between a few individuals or factions takes place. In Bailey's **game theory**, it is an area in which teams that agree on a common set of rules compete.

Band The least complex level of sociocultural integration, associated with hunting-gathering societies. Characterized by small, fluid groups, egalitarianism, informal leadership, and bilateral kinship.

Bivocal symbolism According to Abner Cohen, all true symbols serve both existential and political ends; that is, they are felt in a deeply personal way, but at the same time they maintain political continuity through reaffirming common myths and values.

Chiefdom The least complex form of centralized political system, usually found in cultures that base their subsistence on extensive agriculture or intensive fishing. Characterized by a ranking of individuals and lineages, inheritance of power within a dominant lineage, and maintenance of power through redistribution of wealth by a charismatic chief.

Complementary opposition A system in which groups that are antagonistic at one level will unite at another level to counter a military threat.

Consensual power Leadership that derives from the assent of the people, rather than force alone. This assent may be based on tradition, respect for an office, or faith in the personal qualities of a leader.

Dependent power Power that is granted, allocated, or delegated by someone who holds **independent power.**

Diachronic study An analysis of a society "in time," that is, in a historical or evolutionary context.

Environmental circumscription A theory by Robert Carniero that **primary states** arose when population growth and other pressures within areas bounded by mountains or desert forced increasingly complex modes of political and social organization.

Factions Informal, leader-follower political groups organized for a particular purpose and disbanding when that purpose is accomplished or defeated. See also **Pervasive factionalism** and **Segmentary factional political systems.**

Field The basic unit of study in the **process approach** to political anthropology. Previous researchers tended to focus on a defined group, such as a tribe or community; a field, which is defined anew by each researcher, may cross the boundaries of different groups and may change over time. In Bailey's **game theory,** a "field" is more specifically defined as an area in which rival political structures interact, but without agreed-upon rules between them.

Game theory Introduced into political anthropology by F.G. Bailey, this approach seeks to discover the **normative rules** and **pragmatic rules** of political manipulation. Politics is viewed as a game composed of "teams" competing for "prizes."

General systems theory A relatively new and highly complex paradigm for the social sciences in which whole systems are viewed as adapting to changes in their internal and external environments through feedback mechanisms (see **Positive feedback** and **Negative feedback**). This orientation has been especially important in explaining the rise of primary states.

Hydraulic theory A theory of state formation proposed by Karl Wittfogel. Canal irrigation required a division of classes into workers and administrators and tended to concentrate power in the hands of those who controlled the water supplies upon which the life of the community depended.

Independent power A relation of dominance based on the direct capabilities of an individual, such as his knowledge, skills or personal charisma. In centralized societies, such power may attach to a particular office, such as that of king. See **Dependent power.**

Institutionalization of leadership A theory by Elman Service that the development of centralized political organization can be explained in terms of the perceived benefits of strong leadership and political continuity.

Intensification As used by Marvin Harris, this refers to a fundamental process of cultural evolution by which population pressures combine with resource depletion to force improved means of producing food. Such technological changes in turn require new modes of social organization.

Legitimacy A primary basis for **power** that derives from the people's expectations about the nature of power and how it should be attained, for example, by election in the United States or by holding redistributive feasts in Polynesia.

Negative feedback Deviation-minimizing processes. Change in a system will be limited by other elements of the system so that equilibrium is maintained (e.g., in hot weather the body is cooled by sweating to maintain a constant temperature). See **Positive feedback.**

Neo-evolutionism A revival by Leslie White in the 1940s of 19th-century cultural evolutionary theory. Later theorists distinguished *general evolution*—broad changes in cultural complexity, such as from band to tribal society—and *specific evolution*, the observable adaptational changes of particular societies.

Normative rules In F.G. Bailey's **game theory,** the political rules that are publically professed, such as honesty, sportsmanship, etc. See, in contrast, **Pragmatic rules.**

Pervasive factionalism A condition in which formal political structures have broken down or have become inoperative, and temporary **factions** arise to solve each problem as it appears.

Politics One of those undefinable words that depends on the particular interests of the researcher. A good working definition is as follows: "The processes involved in determining and implementing public goals and . . . the differential achievement and use of power by the members of the group concerned with these goals" (Swartz, Turner and Tuden 1966:7).

Positive feedback Deviation-amplifying processes. A slight "initial kick" will start a process of increasingly rapid change, which will be stopped only when the system attains a new level of equilibrium or collapses. See **Negative feedback.**

Power In its broadest sense, "an ability to influence the behavior of others and/ or gain influence over the control of valued actions" (R. Cohen 1970:31). In its purely political aspect, such influence would be limited to the public domain. This amorphous term is better defined by breaking it into its component parts: **independent power, dependent power, consensual power, legitimacy,** and **support.**

Pragmatic rules In F.G. Bailey's **game theory,** those political rules that are concerned with gaining or maintaining power—i.e., with winning the game— not with public display. See, in contrast, **Normative rules.**

Primary state   A state that developed independently of preexisting states. This occurred in six areas: Mesopotamia, the Nile Valley, the Indus Valley of India, the Yellow River Valley of China, Mesoamerica, and Peru.

Process approach   Sometimes referred to as process theory, though it is too amorphous to constitute a coherent theory. Originally a reaction against **structural functionalism,** this approach emphasizes change and conflict.

Retribalization   The tendency for some tribal groups to become *more* cohesive, to protect economic and political interests, during the process of modernization.

Secondary state   Any state that came into existence through the influence of preexisting states.

Segmentary factional political system   A system either without formal political structures or in which such structures have broken down, so that competition between **factions** becomes the normal mode of political decision-making.

Segmentary lineage   A unilineal system based on small, local, relatively autonomous units that can be put together, building-block fashion, into increasingly larger structures for ritual or military purposes.

State   The most complex level of political integration. Found in societies whose subsistence is based on intensive agriculture, and characterized by leadership centered in an individual or elite group supported by a bureaucracy, suprakinship loyalties, class structure, and economic redistribution based on tribute or taxation.

Structural functionalism   The dominant theoretical orientation of British anthropology during the 1930s and 1940s. **Synchronic study,** usually of groups treated as closed systems, showed how the various component institutions contributed to the equilibrium of the whole.

Support   A broad concept, including virtually anything that contributes to or maintains political **power.** Two basic supports are coercion (force) and **legitimacy.**

Synchronic study   A type of analysis, typical of the **structural functionalists** and French structuralists, that treats societies as though outside of time, i.e., without reference to historical context.

Tribe   A loosely defined term used to denote a wide range of social organizations that exist between hunting-gathering **bands** and centralized systems. Associated with horticulture or pastoralism, charismatic leadership, unilineal kinship, and pantribal sodalities.

Bibliography

Abrahamson, Mark. 1969. "Correlates of Political Complexity." *American Sociological Review* 34:690–701.

Adams, Richard N. 1975. *Energy and Structure: A Theory of Social Power*. Austin: University of Texas Press.

1977 "Power in Human Societies: A Synthesis." In *The Anthropology of Power*, ed. R.D. Fogelson and R.N. Adams. New York: Academic Press.

Adams, Robert McCormick. 1966. *The Evolution of Urban Society*. Chicago: Aldine.

Bailey, F.G. 1960. *Tribe, Caste and Nation*. Manchester: Manchester University Press.

1968 "Parapolitical Systems." In *Local Level Politics*, ed. M. Swartz. Chicago: Aldine.

1969 *Strategems and Spoils: A Social Anthropology of Politics*. New York: Schocken Books.

1970 *Politics and Social Change*. Berkeley: University of California Press.

Balandier, Georges. 1970. *Political Anthropology*. New York: Random House.

Banton, Michael (ed.). 1965. *Political Systems and the Distribution of Power*. London: Tavistock.

Barth, Frederick. 1959. *Political Leadership among the Swat Pathans*. London: Athalone.

Block, Maurice (ed.) . 1975. *Political Language and Oratory in Traditional Society*. New York: Academic Press.

Boas, Franz. 1894. *The Social Organization and Secret Societies of the Kwakiutl Indians*. United States National Museum Annual Report 1894.

Boserup, Esther. 1965. *The Conditions of Agricultural Growth: The Economics of Agrarian Change under Population Pressure.* Chicago: Aldine.

Britan, Gerald M., and Ronald Cohen. 1980. "Toward an Anthropology of Formal Organizations." In *Hierarchy and Society: Anthropological Perspectives on Bureaucracy,* ed. G.M. Britan and R. Cohen. Philadelphia: Institute for the Study of Human Issues.

Britan, Gerald M., and Ronald Cohen (eds.). 1980. *Hierarchy and Society: Anthropological Perspectives on Bureaucracy.* Philadelphia: Institute for the Study of Human Issues.

Buckley, Walter (ed.). 1968. *Modern Systems Research for the Behavioral Sciences: A Sourcebook.* Chicago: Aldine.

Bujra, Janet M. 1973. "The Dynamics of Political Action: A New Look at Factionalism." *American Anthropologist* 75:132–52.

Burling, Robbins. 1974. *The Passage of Power: Studies in Political Succession.* New York: Academic Press.

Campbell, Bernhard G. 1979. *Humankind Emerging,* 2d ed. Boston: Little, Brown.

Carniero, Robert L. 1967. "On the Relationship between Size of Population and Complexity of Social Organization." *Southwestern Journal of Anthropology* 23:234–43.

1970 "A Theory of the Origin of the State." *Science* 169:733–38.

1978 "Political Expansion as an Expression of the Principle of Competitive Exclusion." In *Origins of the State: The Anthropology of Political Evolution,* ed. R. Cohen and E. Service. Philadelphia: Institute for the Study of Human Issues.

Chagnon, Napoleon. 1968. *Yanomamo: The Fierce People.* New York: Holt, Rinehart & Winston.

Childe, V. Gordon. 1936. *Man Makes Himself.* London: Watts.

1946 *What Happened in History.* New York: Penguin.

Claessen, Henri J.M. 1978. "The Early State: A Structural Approach." In *The Early State,* ed. H.J.M. Claessen and Peter Skalník. The Hague, Netherlands: Mouton.

Claessen, Henri J.M., and Peter Skalník. 1978. "The Early State: Theories and Hypotheses." In *The Early State,* ed. H.J.M. Claessen and P. Skalník. The Hague, Netherlands: Mouton.

Claessen, Henri J.M., and Peter Skalník (eds.). 1978. *The Early State.* The Hague, Netherlands: Mouton.

Codere, Helen. 1950. *Fighting with Property: A Study of Kwakiutl Potlatching and Warfare, 1792–1930.* Seattle: University of Washington Press.

1957 "Kwakiutl Society: Rank without Class." *American Anthropologist* 59:473–86.

Cohen, Abner. 1969a. *Custom and Politics in Urban Africa: A Study of Hausa Migrants in a Yoruba Town.* Berkeley: University of California Press.

1969b "Political Anthropology: The Analysis of the Symbolism of Power Relations." *Man* 4:215–44.

1974 *Two-Dimensional Man: An Essay on the Anthropology of Power and Symbolism in Complex Societies.* London: Routledge & Kegan Paul.

1981 *The Politics of Elite Culture: Explorations in the Dramaturgy of Power in a Modern African Society.* Berkeley: University of California Press.

Cohen, Ronald. 1965. "Political Anthropology: The Future of a Pioneer." *Anthropological Quarterly* 38:117–31.

1970 "The Political System." In *A Handbook of Method in Cultural Anthropology,* ed. R. Naroll and R. Cohen. Garden City, N.Y.: Natural History Press.

1978a "Introduction." In *Origins of the State: The Anthropology of Political Evolution,* ed. R. Cohen and E. Service. Philadelphia: Institute for the Study of Human Issues.

1978b "State Foundations: A Controlled Comparison." In *The Origin of the State: The Anthropology of Political Evolution,* ed. R. Cohen and E. Service. Philadelphia: Institute for the Study of Human Issues.

Cohen, Ronald, and John Middleton (eds.). 1967. *Comparative Political Systems: Studies in the Politics of Pre-Industrial Societies.* Austin: University of Texas Press.

Cohen, Ronald, and Alice Schlegal. 1968. "The Tribe as a Socio-Political Unit: A Cross-Cultural Examination." In *Essays on the Problem of Tribe: Proceedings of the 1967 Annual Spring Meeting of the American Ethnological Society,* ed. J. Helm. Seattle: University of Washington Press.

Cohen, Ronald, and Elman Service (eds.). 1978. *Origins of the State: The Anthropology of Political Evolution.* Philadelphia: Institute for the Study of Human Issues.

Colson, Elizabeth. 1968. "Political Anthropology: The Field." In *International Encyclopedia of the Social Sciences,* vol 12, ed. D.L. Sills. New York: Macmillan and Free Press.

1974 *Tradition and Contract: The Problem of Order.* Chicago: Aldine.

Damas, David. 1968. "The Diversity of Eskimo Societies." In *Man, The Hunter,* ed. R.B. Lee and I. DeVore. Chicago: Aldine.

Davenport, W. 1969. "The Hawaiian Cultural Revolution: Some Political and Economic Considerations." *American Anthropologist* 71:1–20.

Deloria, Vine. 1969. *Custer Died for Your Sins.* New York: Avon.

Drucker, P., and Robert F. Heizer. 1967. *To Make My Name Good: A Reexamination of the Southern Kwakiutl Potlatch.* Berkeley: University of California Press.

Dumond, D.E. 1965. "Population Growth and Cultural Change." *Southwestern Journal of Anthropology* 21:302–24.

Easton, David. 1953. *The Political System.* New York: Knopf.

1959 "Political Anthropology." In *Biennial Review of Anthropology, 1958.* Stanford: Stanford University Press.

Eisenstadt, S.N. 1959. "Primitive Political Systems: A Preliminary Comparative Analysis." *American Anthropologist* 61:200–20.

1963 *The Political Systems of Empire.* Glencoe, Ill.: Free Press.

1966 *Modernization: Protest and Change.* Englewood Cliffs. N.J.: Prentice-Hall.

1967 "Transformation of Social, Political, and Cultural Orders in Modernization." In *Comparative Political Systems*, ed. R. Cohen and J. Middleton.
Austin: University of Texas Press.

1970 "Social Change and Development." In *Readings in Social Evolution and
Development*, ed. S.N. Eisenstadt. Oxford: Pergamon Press.

1973 "Varieties of Political Development: The Theoretical Challenge." In *Building States and Nations*, ed. S.N. Eisenstadt and S. Rokkan. Beverly Hills:
Sage.

Engels, Frederick. 1972. *The Origin of the Family, Private Property and the
State*, reprint ed., ed. E.B. Leacock. (Orig. ed. 1891.) New York: International Publishers.

Evans-Pritchard, E.E. 1940a. *The Nuer*. Oxford: Oxford University Press.

1940b "The Nuer of the Southern Sudan." In *African Political Systems*, ed. M.
Fortes and E.E. Evans-Pritchard. Oxford: Oxford University Press.

Faron, L.C. 1967. "The Mapuche Reservation as a Political Unit." In *Comparative
Political Systems*, ed. R. Cohen and J. Middleton. Austin: University of
Texas Press.

Flannery, Kent. 1968. "Archeological Systems Theory and Early Mesoamerica."
In *Anthropological Archeology in the Americas*, ed. B. Meggers. Washington, D.C.: Anthropological Society of Washington.

Fogelson, R.D., and Richard N. Adams (eds.). 1977. *The Anthropology of Power:
Ethnographic Studies from Asia, Oceania, and the New World*. New York:
Academic Press.

Fortes, Meyer, and E.E. Evans-Pritchard (eds.). 1940. *African Political Systems*.
Oxford: Oxford University Press.

Frazer, James G. 1900. *The Golden Bough*, 3 vols. (Orig. ed. 1890.) London:
Macmillan.

Freeman, L.C., and R.F. Winch. 1957. "Societal Complexity: An Empirical Test
of a Typology of Societies." *American Journal of Sociology* 62:461–66.

Fried, Morton H. 1967. *The Evolution of Political Society*. New York: Random
House.

1968 "On the Concepts of 'Tribe' and 'Tribal Society.' " In *Essays on the Problem of Tribe: Proceedings of the 1967 Annual Spring Meeting of the American Ethnological Society*, ed. J. Helm. Seattle: University of Washington
Press.

1978 "The State, the Chicken, and the Egg: Or, What Came First?" In *Origins
of the State*, ed. R. Cohen and E. Service. Philadelphia: Institute for the
Study of Human Issues.

Fulton, Richard. 1972. "The Political Structure and Function of Poro in Kpelle
Society." *American Anthropologist* 74:1218–33.

Gluckman, Max. 1940. "The Kingdom of the Zulu of South Africa." In *African
Political Systems*, ed. M. Fortes and E.E. Evans-Pritchard. Oxford: Oxford
University Press.

1960 *Order and Rebellion in Tribal Africa*. Glencoe, Ill.: Free Press.

1965 *Politics, Law and Ritual in Tribal Society*. Oxford: Basil Blackwell.

1969 *Custom and Conflict in Africa.* New York: Barnes & Noble.

Gluckman, Max, and Fred Eggan. 1965. "Introduction." In *Political Systems and the Distribution of Power,* ed. M. Banton. London: Tavistock.

Goody, Jack (ed.). 1966. *Succession to High Office.* Cambridge: Cambridge University Press.

Harner, Michael. 1970. "Population Pressure and the Social Evolution of Agriculturalists." *Southwestern Journal of Anthropology* 26:67–86.

Harris, Marvin. 1968. *The Rise of Anthropological Theory.* New York: Thomas Crowell Co.

1974 *Cows, Pigs, Wars and Witches.* New York: Vintage.

1977 *Cannibals and Kings: The Origins of Culture.* New York: Vintage.

Helm, J. (ed.). 1968. *Essays on the Problem of Tribe: Proceedings of the 1967 Annual Spring Meeting of the American Ethnological Society.* Seattle: University of Washington Press.

Hoebel, E. Adamson. 1940. *The Political Organization and Law Ways of the Comanche Indians.* American Anthropological Association Memoir 54.

1960 *The Cheyenne: Indians of the Great Plains.* New York: Holt, Rinehart & Winston.

Huizer, Gerrit, and Bruce Mannheim (eds.). 1979. *The Politics of Anthropology: From Colonialism and Sexism toward a View from Below.* The Hague, Netherlands: Mouton.

Hunt, Eva, and Robert C. Hunt. 1978. "Irrigation, Conflict and Politics: A Mexican Case." In *Origins of the State,* ed. R. Cohen and E. Service. Philadelphia: Institute for the Study of Human Issues.

Izmirlian, Harry, Jr. 1969. "Structural and Decision-Making Models: A Political Example." *American Anthropologist* 71:1062–73.

Janssen, Jacobus J. 1978. "The Early State in Ancient Egypt." In *The Early State,* ed. H.J.M. Claessen and P. Skalník. The Hague, Netherlands: Mouton.

Jolly, Clifford J., and Fred Plog. 1976. *Physical Anthropology and Archeology,* 2d ed. New York: Knopf.

Kuper, Adam. 1973. *Anthropologists and Anthropology: The British School, 1922–1972.* New York: Pica Press.

Leach, Edmund R. 1954. *Political Systems of Highland Burma.* Boston: Beacon Press.

1961 *Rethinking Anthropology.* London: Athlone Press.

Leacock, Eleanor B. 1979. "Lewis Henry Morgan on Government and Property." In *New Directions in Political Economy: An Approach from Anthropology,* ed. M.B. Leons and F. Rothstein. Westport, Conn.: Greenwood Press.

Levinson, David, and Martin J. Malone. 1980. *Toward Explaining Human Culture: A Critical Review of the Findings of Worldwide Cross-Cultural Research.* New Haven, Conn.: HRAF Press.

Lewellen, Ted C. 1978. *Peasants in Transition: The Changing Economy of the Peruvian Aymara.* Boulder, Colo.: Westview Press.

1979 "Deviant Religion and Cultural Evolution: The Aymara Case." *Journal for the Scientific Study of Religion* 18:243–51.

1981 "Political Anthropology." In *The Handbook of Political Behavior*, vol. 3, ed. S. Long. New York: Plenum.

Lewis, Herbert. 1968. "Typology and Process in Political Evolution." In *Essays on the Problem of Tribe: Proceedings of the 1967 Annual Spring Meeting of the American Ethnological Society*, ed. J. Helm. Seattle: University of Washington Press.

Little, Kenneth. 1965. "The Political Function of Poro." *Africa* 35:349–65.

Lloyd, Peter C. 1965. "The Political Structure of African Kingdoms: An Explanatory Model." In *Political Systems and the Distribution of Power*, ed. M. Banton. London: Tavistock.

Logan, N., and W. Sanders. 1976. "The Model." In *The Valley of Mexico*, ed. E. Wolf. Albuquerque: University of New Mexico Press.

Lomax, Alan, and C.M. Arensberg. 1977. "A Worldwide Evolutionary Classification of Cultures by Subsistence Systems." *Current Anthropology* 18:659–708.

Lomax, Alan, and Norman Berkowitz. 1972. "The Evolutionary Taxonomy of Culture." *Science* 177:228–39.

Lowie, Robert H. 1962. *The Origin of the State*. (Orig. ed. 1927.) New York: Russell & Russell.

1970 *Primitive Society*. (Orig. ed. 1920.) New York: Liveright.

Maine, Henry. 1887. *Ancient Law: Its Connection with the Early History of Society and Its Relation to Modern Ideas*. (Orig. ed. 1861.) London: J. Murray.

Mair, Lucy P. 1962. *Primitive Government*. Baltimore: Penguin.

Malinowski, Bronislaw. 1922. *Argonauts of the Western Pacific*. New York: Dutton.

Marquet, Jacques. 1971. *Power and Society in Africa*. New York: McGraw-Hill.

Marshall, Lorna. 1967. "!Kung Bushman Bands." In *Comparative Political Systems*, ed. R. Cohen and J. Middleton. Austin: University of Texas Press.

Mason, J. Alden. 1957. *The Ancient Civilizations of Peru*. Middlesex, U.K.: Penguin.

McLean, John. 1889. "The Blackfoot Sun Dance." *Proceedings of the Canadian Institute*, ser. 3, vol. 4:231–37.

Middleton, John. 1960. *Lugbara Religion: Ritual and Authority among an East African People*. London: Oxford University Press.

1966 "The Resolution of Conflict among the Lugbara of Uganda." In *Political Anthropology*, ed. M. Swartz, V. Turner, and A. Tuden. Chicago: Aldine.

Middleton, John, and David Tate (eds.). 1958. *Tribes without Rulers*. London: Routledge & Kegan Paul.

Mitchell, Clyde. 1964. "Foreword." In *The Politics of Kinship: A Study of Social Manipulation among the Lakeside Tonga*, by J. van Velsen. Manchester: Manchester University Press.

Morgan, Lewis Henry. 1877. *Ancient Society*. New York: Henry Holt.

Murdock, George Peter. 1949. *Social Structure*. New York: Macmillan.

1959 "Evolution in Social Organization." In *Evolution and Anthropology: A*

Centennial Appraisal, ed. B. Meggers. Washington, D.C.: Anthropological Society of Washington.

1973 "Measurement and Cultural Complexity." *Ethnology* 12:379–92.

Murdock, George Peter, and Suzanne F. Wilson. 1972. "Settlement Patterns and Community Organization: Cross-Cultural Codes 2." *Ethnology* 11:254–95.

Murra, John V. 1958. "On Inca Political Structure." In *Systems of Political Control and Bureaucracy in Human Societies: Proceedings of the 1958 Annual Spring Meeting of the American Ethnological Society*. Seattle: University of Washington Press.

Nicholas, Ralph W. 1965. "Factions: A Comparative Analysis." In *Political Systems and the Distribution of Power*, ed. M. Banton. London: Tavistock.

1966 "Segmentary Factional Political Systems." In *Political Anthropology*, ed. M. Swartz, V. Turner, and A. Tuden. Chicago: Aldine.

Ornstein, Henry. 1980. "Asymmetrical Reciprocity: A Contribution to the Theory of Political Legitimacy." *Current Anthropology* 21:69–91.

Otterbein, Keith P. 1971. "Comment on 'Correlates of Political Complexity.' " *American Sociological Review* 36:113–14.

Paige, Jeffrey M. 1974. "Kinship and Polity in Stateless Societies." *American Journal of Sociology* 80:301–20.

Patterson, Thomas C. 1971. "The Emergence of Food Production in Central Peru." In *Prehistoric Agriculture*, ed. S. Struever. Garden City, N.Y.: Natural History Press.

Pfeiffer, John E. 1977. *The Emergence of Society: A Prehistory of the Establishment*. New York: McGraw Hill.

Price, Barbara J. 1978. "Secondary State Formation: An Explanatory Model." In *Origins of the State*, ed. R. Cohen and E. Service. Philadelphia: Institute for the Study of Human Issues.

1979 "Turning States' Evidence: Problems in the Theory of State Formation." In *New Directions in Political Economy: An Approach from Anthropology*, ed. M.B. Leons and F. Rothstein. Westport, Conn.: Greenwood Press.

Radcliffe-Brown, A.R. 1940. "Preface." In *African Political Systems*, ed. M. Fortes and E.E. Evans-Pritchard, Oxford: Oxford University Press.

Rappaport, Roy. 1968. *Pigs for the Ancestors: Ritual in the Ecology of a New Guinea People*. New Haven, Conn.: Yale University Press.

Rostow, W. 1960. *The Stages of Economic Growth*. Cambridge: Cambridge University Press.

Schwartz, Norman B. 1969. "Goal Attainment through Factionalism: A Guatemalan Case." *American Anthropologist* 71:1088–1108.

Sahlins, Marshall. 1969. "The Segmentary Lineage and Predatory Expansion." *American Anthropologist* 63:332–45.

Sahlins, Marshall, and Elman Service. 1960. *Evolution and Culture*. Ann Arbor: University of Michigan Press.

Schapera, Isaac. 1967. *Government and Politics in Tribal Societies*. New York: Schocken Books.

Seaton, S. Lee. 1978. "The Early State in Hawaii." In *The Early State,* ed. H.J.M. Claessen and P. Skalník. The Hague, Netherlands: Mouton.

Seaton, S. Lee, and Henri J.M. Claessen (eds.). 1979. *Political Anthropology: The State of the Art.* The Hague, Netherlands: Mouton.

Service, Elman R. 1962. *Primitive Social Organization: An Evolutionary Perspective,* 2d ed. New York: Random House.

  1975 *Origins of the State and Civilization: The Processes of Cultural Evolution.* New York: W.W. Norton.

  1978 "Classical and Modern Theories of Government." In *Origins of the State: The Anthropology of Political Evolution,* ed. R. Cohen and E. Service. Philadelphia: Institute for the Study of Human Issues.

Siegel, B.J., and A.R. Beals. 1960. "Pervasive Factionalism." *American Anthropologist* 62:394–417.

Smith, Michael G. 1968. "Political Anthropology: Political Organization." In *International Encyclopedia of the Social Sciences,* vol. 12, ed. D.L. Sills. New York: Macmillan and the Free Press.

Southall, Aidan W. 1953. *Alur Society.* Cambridge: W. Heffer & Sons.

  1965 "A Critique of the Typology of States and Political Systems." In *Political Systems and the Distribution of Power,* ed. M. Banton. London: Tavistock.

  1974 "State Formation in Africa." In *Annual Review of Anthropology,* vol. 3, ed. B.J. Siegel. Palo Alto, Cal.: Annual Reviews, Inc.

Southwold, Martin. 1966. "Succession to the Throne in Buganda." In *Succession to High Office,* ed. J. Goody. Cambridge: Cambridge University Press.

Spier, Leslie. 1921. *The Sun Dance of the Plains Indians: Its Development and Diffusion.* American Museum of Natural History Anthropological Papers, vol. 16, pt. 7.

Spiro, Melford E. 1965. "A Typology of Social Structure and the Patterning of Social Distributions: A Cross-Cultural Study." *American Anthropologist* 67:1097–1119.

Stern, Bernhard J. 1931. *Lewis Henry Morgan: Social Evolutionist.* Chicago: University of Chicago Press.

Stevenson, Robert R. 1968. *Population and Political Systems in Tropical Africa.* New York: Columbia University Press.

Steward, Julian. 1949. "Cultural Complexity and Law: A Trial Formulation of the Development of Early Civilizations." *American Anthropologist* 51:1–27.

  1955 *Theory of Culture Change: The Methodology of Multilinear Evolution.* Urbana: University of Illinois Press.

Swartz, Marc. 1968. *Local-Level Politics.* Chicago: Aldine.

Swartz, Marc, Victor Turner, and Arthur Tuden (eds.). 1966. *Political Anthropology.* Chicago: Aldine.

Textor, Robert B. 1967. *A Cross-Cultural Summary.* New Haven: HRAF Press.

Tuden, Arthur, and Catherine Marshall. 1972. "Political Organization: Cross-Cultural Codes 4." *Ethnology* 11:436–64.

Turner, Victor. 1957. *Schism and Continuity in an African Society.* Manchester: Manchester University Press.

van Velsen, J. 1964. *The Politics of Kinship: A Study in Social Manipulation among the Lakeside Tonga*. Manchester: Manchester University Press.

Vincent, Joan. 1978. "Political Anthropology: Manipulative Strategies." In *Annual Review of Anthropology*, vol. 7, ed. B.J. Siegal. Glencoe, Calif.: Annual Reviews, Inc.

Voget, Fred W. 1975. *A History of Ethnology*. New York: Holt, Rinehart & Winston.

Weatherford, J. McIver. 1981. *Tribes on the Hill*. New York: Rawson, Wade.

Wenke, Robert J. 1980. *Patterns in Prehistory: Mankind's First Three Million Years*. New York: Oxford University Press.

Weyer, E.M. 1959. "The Structure of Social Organization among the Eskimo." In *Comparative Political Systems*, ed. R. Cohen and J. Middleton. Austin: University of Texas Press.

White, Leslie. 1943. "Energy and the Evolution of Culture." *American Anthropologist* 45:335–56.

  1949 *The Science of Culture*. New York: Grove.

  1959 *The Evolution of Culture*. New York: McGraw Hill.

Whyte, Martin King. 1980. "Bureaucracy and Anti-Bureaucracy in the People's Republic of China." In *Hierarchy and Society: Anthropological Perspectives on Bureaucracy*, ed. Gerald M. Britan and Ronald Cohen. Philadelphia: Institute for the Study of Human Issues.

Winkler, Edwin A. 1970. "Political Anthropology." In *Biennial Review of Anthropology, 1969*. Stanford: Stanford University Press.

Wirsing, Rolf. 1973. "Political Power and Information: A Cross-Cultural Study." *American Anthropologist* 75:153–70.

Wissler, Clark. 1918. *The Sun Dance of the Blackfoot Indians*. Anthropological Papers of the American Museum of Natural History, vol. 16, pt. 3.

Wittfogel, Karl. 1957. *Oriental Despotism: A Comparative Study of Total Power*. New Haven: Yale University Press.

Wolf, Eric R., and Edward Hansen. 1972. *The Human Condition in Latin America*. New York: Oxford University Press.

Wright, Henry T. 1977. "Recent Research on the Origin of the State." In *Annual Review of Anthropology, 1977*, ed. B.J. Siegel. Palo Alto, Calif.: Annual Reviews, Inc.

  1978 "Toward an Explanation of the Origin of the State." In *Origins of the State: The Anthropology of Political Evolution*. Philadelphia: Institute for the Study of Human Issues.

Index